A Luftwaffe Bomber Pilot Remembers

A Luftwaffe Bomber Pilot Remembers

World War II from the Cockpit

Klaus Häberlen

Schiffer Military History
Atglen, PA

DEDICATION

This book is dedicated to my dear wife, Liesel, to my comrades in arms with whom I flew more than 300 missions, and to my brother, Walter, who as fighter pilot died on 20 April 1945.

Book Design by Ian Robertson.
Copyright © 2001 by Klaus Häberlen.
Library of Congress Control Number: 2001090045

Printed in the United States of America.
ISBN: 0-7643-1393-2

We are interested in hearing from authors with book ideas on related topics.

Published by Schiffer Publishing Ltd.
4880 Lower Valley Road
Atglen, PA 19310
Phone: (610) 593-1777
FAX: (610) 593-2002
E-mail: Schifferbk@aol.com.
Visit our web site at: www.schifferbooks.com
Please write for a free catalog.
This book may be purchased from the publisher.
Please include $3.95 postage.
Try your bookstore first.

In Europe, Schiffer books are distributed by:
Bushwood Books
6 Marksbury Avenue
Kew Gardens
Surrey TW9 4JF
England
Phone: 44 (0) 20 8392-8585
FAX: 44 (0) 20 8392-9876
E-mail: Bushwd@aol.com.
Free postage in the UK. Europe: air mail at cost.
Try your bookstore first.

Contents

INTRODUCTION

After living under three different regimes, and after eighty years enduring the negatively biased opinions of the armed forces under Hitler as described in the media, by persons with little or no knowledge of the true facts, the idea was born that a book written by someone who experienced this period was necessary to put things in a true perspective.

It is true that some career officers agreed with Hitler's policy, but in the main, this was not generally true with the majority of officers.

The latest defamation of our armed forces by a Federal High Court, was to state that soldiers were murderers. At the same time, an exhibition was touring Germany with the theme "War of Extermination, Crimes of the Deutsche Wehrmacht." It was organized by the multi-millionaire Reemstma. What was not mentioned, was that Reemstma earned his millions during the Hitler period selling cigarettes to the Army. This was a virtual monopoly.

I have written my book from my many memories, photographs, and my flight log book. Everything I write, happened. I have written only what I consider to be of interest, and necessary.

Maybe my book will help the reader obtain a better understanding of my generation.

My special thanks go to my comrade, Dietrich Widmann, who checked the complete text.

1

YOUTH AND SCHOOL YEARS

I was born on 14 April 1916 in Geislingen, Wuerttemberg. It lies on the main railway line Stuttgart-Ulm-Munich. I was lucky in that I grew up in a large family with three brothers. My father came from Esslingen, where his father owned a large chemist's shop. He died in 1918, and my grandmother then sold the shop, together with a large block of flats, since she was not in a position to administer them. She invested the money in government bonds, and lost it all during the depression of 1922/23. Father's sister, Margrit, whose husband died in the war, lived with my grandmother and helped to support her as she held a position as a teacher in the high school. Of course, my father helped, as well. My mother came from the island of Ruegen. Her father held the position as legal advisor to the county court in Bergen. She lost her parents at an early age and grew up with relatives. She was staying with an aunt in Tuebingen when she met my father, who was studying law at Tuebingen university.

The family lived in a rented flat in the district of Altenstadt. Here my memory of this time fails me, but from hearsay, I learned of an event that happened in 1918.

Our flat was near the Wuerttembergischen Metallwarenfabrik, well known for the manufacture of quality tableware. During the 1914/18 war it was converted to a munitions factory. One day a French aircraft bombed the factory. The sirens sounded, and then the bombs fell. At the same time my sister, with me in a pram, was at the front of the house. She knew that during an air attack one should take shelter in a cellar. To this end, she ran to a cellar, and she, and the pram with me in it, tumbled into the cellar. When later in life I would do something silly, I was told that since that tumble into the cellar—during which I fell on my head—I must have suffered some brain damage.

With the help of relatives, my mother bought a small house for the parents in the Karlstrasse, near the factory. From the house one had a splendid view over the "Five valleys town" of Geislingen. My first memory of the house was the gas lighting and the coal oven that often smoked, and left a lot of ashes which had to be cleared away. Later we obtained electricity, and several years later, our house was the first to have central heating installed. Our double story house had a pointed roof. Hence, the top story had sloping walls in most of the rooms. From the entrance door were steps which led to the garden, and on the slope leading to the street were two tall birch trees and bushes. In front of the side door was a level lawn where our garden chairs were available. There was also a sand box for playing in. Behind the house was the Zeppelinstrasse, which was the boundary for our berry bushes and vegetable garden.

On the ground floor was a large dining room, a drawing-room, and a library, together with a small verandah. Above the verandah, on the next floor, was our balcony. Facing the vegetable garden was a large kitchen with a larder. It had a rear entrance door and a verandah.

On the first floor were the parent's bedroom, children's bedroom, and a play room. There were also two other small rooms and the bathroom. In the finished attic were also rooms, with a guest room at the front, and on the garden side two small rooms. Altogether, a large house.

I remember my last year in kindergarten very well. The rooms bordered on a house that belonged to the Machine Factory, Geislingen (MAG).

Our nursery-school teacher, Miss Stehlin, was the daughter of the director of the factory. She often showed us the trout that played in the nearby stream. We were also allowed to feed the fish with leftovers from our breakfast bread. That was, for me, always an experience.

On my way to the kindergarten I was accompanied by two older children who made my life hell, especially when playing in the street. In those days, one could play in the street.

No cars were on the street; only the farmer's horse-drawn wagons were to be seen on their way to and from town. I had a scooter, which I was only able to use when I begged my mother for apples or sweets that I could give to my "playmates." The parents of my playmates were not in a position to buy a scooter for their children. I suffered under them until the end of the infants school, until I found a way to resist them. I was just six years old when I started infants school. There I met Hans, the son of my father's good friend, Mr. Muff. We quickly became good friends. Our teacher was an elderly man who would soon be pensioned off. No one respected him, and rowdies in the class took advantage of this. I was one of the best three pupils in the class, and we were allowed to move from the third class of the basic school to the high school without taking the entrance exam.

The high school had two learning directions: one was where English and French were studied for one year; and the other was where English and French were studied from the beginning, and later Latin was studied. We joined the latter class, where I had difficulty, while the jump from the third class to high school was expecting too much. I stayed a little longer in the sixth class! The friendship with Hans continued, but was not so prevalent. Next to me in the classroom sat Ernst Alexander, and we soon became friends. This friendship exists to this day, and while Ernst lives not too far away, we see each other often. He was the best pupil in the class, and as such, often helped me with difficult problems. He lived in Deggingen, and traveled by train to school. When we had afternoon school he would often eat with us, and later we would work on homework together in my room.

2

HIGHLIGHTS OF MY YOUTH

I will not discuss too much concerning school, since the family was more important in my youth. I had two sisters and a brother. The eldest child was named Ursula, but was called Ursel. Next in line was myself, followed by my other sister, Hanna, and lastly, my brother, Walter, who was called Wagge.

There was a difference of eleven years between Ulla and Wagge, and so it came that the two older children had left home while the two younger children were still attending school. Due to the age differences we all had separate rooms. Both Ulla and I left home at the age of nineteen. On the ground floor of the house was a large dining room, my father's office, and the parlor, which was only used when visitors came. Eleven o'clock on Sundays was the accepted time for visitors. These were people newly moved into the area, such as newlyweds lawyers, and even judges—people of some standing in society. When evening dinner guests were expected, the door between the dining room and parlor was opened.

We children were also expected to help with garden work, to begin with, weeding. Later, I had to mow the lawn in front of the house. We earned 10 Pfennige per hour. This was in addition to the 50 Pfennige weekly pocket money. Not all schoolchildren were given pocket money, although some did get more than us.

I had a good understanding with my sister Ursula. She helped me a lot with school work, because she was a good student than I was. Later, when I joined the Youth Movement, she joined the "Ring Saint George," a girls' organization in which she remained until the end of school exams.

For us it was a duty to be employed and work for a business, and my sister reached the position of stores overseer in a storage hall.

Between my other sister, Hanna, and me, things were not so harmonious. She often told tales to my parents, mainly about things that she thought I would not tell my parents. I still remember when she told our parents why I was late one time for the evening meal. She piped up, "I know why Klaus is late. He was with Liesel under the lamp by father's office." I immediately sprang up and gave her a clout before my mother could intervene. The result was that I had to go to my room, without my evening meal.

My brother Wagge was just ten years old when I became a soldier. He had only two interests in life; one was jazz music, and the other was the desire to become a pilot, following me, in that I transferred to the Air Force in 1936.

I have most pleasant memories of weekends spent with my parents. We would walk miles exploring the area around the nearby Geislingen and the Schwaebischen Alb. Once a month I was not at home on the weekend due to duties in the youth movement. Often my mother stayed at home to look after the younger children. Our walks in the Schwarzwald will always remain in my memory. During the autumn of 1928 we traveled by train to Titisee, then walked over the Feldberg and through the Schoenauer valley, where we finally reached Todtnau and spent the night in the cafe Schlageter.

Schlageter was executed by the French occupying army for blowing up military transports. Since then he has been acclaimed as a hero. His parents owned a cafe in Todtnau, where a monument to his memory exists in the market square. His life impressed me very much.

Our walking travels continued to Saeckingen, and from there we walked along the River Rhine to Laufenburg, where we spent the night. In the morning we caught the train to the Rhine waterfall, in Schaffhausen. That year it had rained heavily, so that the waterfall was more impressive than when less rain had fallen. Later we took a motorboat ride to Stein-on-the-Rhine where we stayed the night. The next day we took a Rhine motor ship to Constance, and then we traveled on the newly opened ferry on lake Constance, to Meersburg. We continued on foot to Friedrichshafen. The way was used by the wine growers going to the slopes on which the grape-vines grew. On the steep hillsides grew the grapes for the well-known Meersburger wine. Now and again a gap between the vines allowed fruit to be grown. On the way there was a small stream which flowed into the lake. We had reached Hagnau. On the first slope we came to was a wine grower who was emptying a basket of grapes into a large container. As he saw me, he gave me a large bunch of grapes, for which we thanked him. As we could not eat all of the grapes, we put them in our rucksack. We then came to a newly opened hotel, in front of which stood the owner. My father asked if a certain sort of wine called "Suser" was available; the answer was yes, so we went in for breakfast. As we were the only guests, the owner sat with us after we were served. My mother had often expressed a wish to live by the lake, and this led to my father asking the hotel owner if he knew of a suitable plot of building land near the water that was for sale. The hotel owner's brother had a suitable plot which he wanted to sell. After we got directions to the brother's house, we made our way there. Great was our surprise, as the brother turned out to be the wine grower who had given us the grapes. The plot of land turned out to be the slope which we had seen as we received the grapes, therefore, there was no need for further viewing. We quickly made our way to Friedrichshafen, where we caught a train to Geislingen. The very next morning my parents traveled to Hagnau and bought the plot. We learned later that it was one of very few plots which bordered on the water. This later became our second home.

My father had often accompanied his mother on holidays as a child in Schruns, in Montafon. He was from childhood a devoted mountain climber. He knew all the block huts and mountains in Austria which could be climbed without being in a group of people. In Geislingen he was chairman of the earlier "German Austria Alps club." He had belonged to this club since his student days. I also joined this club when I was 14 years old. As my father knew his way around in Montafon, we, that is, the two older children and our father, did not spend much time in the hotel, as we were most of the time in the mountains. Mother remained in the hotel with the two younger children. Father, Ulla, and I made our first stop at the guest house in St. Anton in Arlberg, where we breakfasted. Every day at dawn we sallied forth to visit as many of the club's block-huts that were not too far away. Ulla was often not in the mood to go walking, so she stayed at our first stop, the guest-house in St. Anton, with the patron's daughter. After we had climbed the Sulzfluh mountain, father decided that we would climb the Pateriol, one of the most attractive mountains in the Arlberg. It was similar to the Matterhorn in Switzerland. It was for me an attractive proposition to climb such a mountain. With a qualified guide, we walked on a summer's day to the Konstanzer guest house, which was on the mountain. There father booked us a double room, and for the guide, a single room. I will never forget a saying that the guide told us after the evening meal as he ordered a glass of wine. My father asked him if in the morning he would be fit after so much wine, and he answered, "Doctor, when wine is enjoyed in moderate amounts, it does not hurt to drink large amounts."

We breakfasted at four o'clock in the morning and then set off. The climb was very difficult, since the way led over steep incline covered with loose schale. This meant that with every step forward, one slipped half a step backwards. Although the guide carried both our rucksacks, it was hard going for both of us. After climbing for four hours, we reached the rock cliffs. The going was much easier, and the route had signposts. About 150 m below the summit a chimney some 30 to 40 m high had to be climbed. As there were steps and handholds conveniently spaced, it was not too difficult. The guide went first, followed by my father, and I brought up the rear. Above the rocks we were roped together, which was for me a new experience. We had just started climbing the chimney when my father let out a cry of pain. While reaching up for a hand hold, he had put his right arm out of joint. This was an injury that he first had when he was a student, during fencing. It had happened often since then, and the shoulder was "worn-out." My father knew of this injury, so he sat on a convenient ledge where the guide secured him with a rope, and he then took father's arm and pulled until his shoulder was again in place. He then bound his arm to his side with a bandage he had in his first-aid bag. Father had taken a pain killer tablet, and we sat there until it began to take effect. Suddenly, I became afraid, and I cried that I did not want to go forward or backwards. The guide calmed me down, and roped together, with me in the lead, we came down the chimney, and eventually, to the guest house. The owner contacted the Red Cross who, with a suitable vehicle, brought Father to a doctor. My father was used to this, but it filled me with unrest.

As chairman of the "German Austrian Alps Club" in Geislingen, my father had for a long time worked to obtain our own block hut in the Alps. A while after our holiday in St. Anton was over, we received the news that an area at the end of the Bregenzer forest was at our disposal. The next holiday arrived, and my parents, with me and Wagge, went to the hotel Mohnenfluh in Schroecken. It lay at the foot of the Hochtannbergpass, which led into the Lechtal. With us were the family Hohlfeld, who were also staying at the same hotel. Mr. Hohlfeld was the technical director at a cotton mill in Kuchen, where, after the war, I learned a trade. Father and I, together with the family Hohlfeld, wandered through the area where the block hut was situated, and the nearby 2,450 m mountain named Braunarlspitze. We climbed it together, while mother stayed in the valley with Wagge.

From Schroecken, we began the climb of the Widderstein mountain. It is 2,600 m high. One can also start climbing from Ritzlern. From the peak we climbed over the Hochkrumbach, and on the way back we wandered by the pretty lake Koeber, in the direction of Schroecken. The last tour with my father was from Schroecken, past the lake Koeber, and to the "Goldenen Berg" hotel. It belonged to a friend of my father, and had recently opened. This tour had taken some 10 hours of steady walking.

My father was among the few people who could name almost all of the peaks. He knew his way around better than most of the locals in Montafon, Vorarlberg, and the Tirol. He knew all the train connections, every street, and every pass. He knew, too, what was worth seeing, as before every journey he studied all the necessary literature. I tried to reach the same level, but never succeeded.

3

HIGH SCHOOL AND HARD TIMES

Our school was divided into three levels, the lowest level being on the ground floor, the middle level on the first floor, and the third level on the second floor. French was taught until the 4th class, thereafter Latin was taught, and after the 7th class, English. Up to the examination time there were 30 pupils, many of which, after the exams, entered a trade training scheme or a further education scheme. Some pupils stayed on in the school, nine in my class. We would take the higher examination later. I was not too bad in French, but Latin was a weak subject for me, mainly due to the grammar, which I found horrible. Math was also a somewhat weak point with me. This was evident later when I had problems in physics. English I did not find too difficult. My favorite subjects were history, German, geography, and sport. While I was engaged in activities to do with the youth organization, little time was left for school work. I, therefore, just managed to pass the exams. My school report often carried the remark "Should work harder," or, "Final exams in danger."

Attendance at a higher school meant that school fees were necessary. Only really "bright" pupils were exempted, and school fees were paid monthly. I remember that in the first school year every pupil brought money from home. The beginning of the thirties saw a change. This was due to the recession, which had made many workers redundant. Of course, many pupils could not pay the required fee then, and therefore had to leave the school.

As a result of the vast unemployment, it came to pass that many schoolchildren were given only a piece of bread to eat in the interval, since the money just was not there.

When one compares today's "poor" people who receive social help with those of my generation, then more than half of the children were poor.

As a result of the hard times, which I lived through, many political parties sprang up overnight, with both left and right orientation. Until the beginning of 1933 our school remained undisturbed. Our teacher in history was Dr. Glueck, a very reasonable sort of person. He taught about the periods before, during, and after the first world war. He held the view that the Treaty of Versailles was an act of revenge, and he admired the then foreign minister who tried to minimize the effects of the treaty. In the classroom, he was neutral with regard to political parties, even after Hitler's take over. He did not agree with Hitler's policies, but was in no position to alter anything. Until 1933 none of the teaching staff had discussed the political situation, not even when their salaries were reduced due to lack of government funds. Although they received smaller salaries, they could not be described as poor.

4

MY TIME IN THE YOUTH MOVEMENT

I was in the second class in the high school when a pupil from the fourth class asked me if I was interested in spending an evening at his home with others. Guenter Groschopf was the son of a doctor, and due to his rather small figure, he was known as "Stump." He had organized a "Youth group" in Geislingen. After I had obtained my parents' permission I was able to visit this group. I was filled with enthusiasm as we sang songs about wandering, and from the tales about the country people's war in the middle ages. I was also introduced to Morse code. My parents allowed me to join the group. The group belonged to the "Ring St. George" with headquarters in Tuebingen. There were many other groups in Wuerttemberg. A captain, who was wounded in the war and discharged, led the "Ring St. George," which was also affiliated with the German Youth Movement. Because of this, members of different groups were able to meet and get to know one another during the singing, wandering, and traveling which we did together. We also learned a lot about nature and our country. The group had existed before the first world war and had no political background. Contact with foreign organizations, such as the scout movement, also existed.

In the "Ring St. George" we did not use our names. We were given old Germanic names instead. Mine was Alarich. Other names, such as Hagen, Gunter, and Siegfried were also in use. The group met every week, and once a month we had a weekend outing. During the holidays we camped and used the time to get to know the countryside and each other. Each year we camped in a different area. We also had a flag; it was black with a blue lily, which was the symbol of the youth movement. During this time I came to know the legendary Thomas Laerner. He organized the youth movement after the war with contacts in Finland, Russia, and the Baltic States. He had the vision of uniting the youth of every country. During the war from 1939 to 1945 he left Germany. He reappeared in the D.D.R., where he organized the "Free German Youth." That his vision was never realized was due, as with so many visions, that it did not fit in with the political views of the time, and were ignored by the politicians of the day.

It came about that our youth leader "Stump" left Geislingen to take up an apprenticeship, and I took his place as youth leader for our 12 members. In the summer of 1930 I had to go to Erbach, on the river Neckar, to a group leader's camp. The first evening was a discussion over a visit to Finland, which was planned for the autumn. At the campfire the cost was discussed, and it was decided that a per head cost of Reichmark 80 was what every member must pay. The cost for board and lodging was additional. I made the suggestion that the "better-off" parents should pay a little more money, which would allow the members with parents who were not so well-off to make the proposed trip. I was disappointed when my suggestion was flatly rejected. We had two army tents that slept 12 persons. After the campfire discussion ended we turned in. I did not sleep, but waited until the others were asleep. I then packed my things and left a note saying that I was leaving the group, because I did not want anything to do with such unsociable people. Just after midnight, I mounted my bicycle and rode through the Neckar valley, in the direction of home. After several hours I had almost reached Stuttgart, and I was at the end of my strength. I collected what little money I had and bought a train ticket. I did not have enough money to buy a ticket to Geislingen, but went as far as I possibly could. The last few miles I went on foot. I eventually reached home very tired and exhausted. Later attempts to change my mind were useless. The group then came to a decision, the meaning and effect of which we could not foresee.

I knew the leader of the Geislinger Hitler youth. He came to our house to carry out repairs, and when he was finished we had a long talk. I asked him if he could help us, that is, the members of our group whose ages were under 14, to form a youth group associated with the "Ring St. George." A few days later he let me know that my plan was acceptable. The whole group, therefore, transferred to the "German Youth." This would, after the end of the war, bring me a lot of problems. In 1934 I decided to leave the youth movement, in order to study for the final school exams. I received the "Golden Hitler Youth Medal" for my work in the youth movement, which, after the war, was the reason I was accused of being a political activist in the Nazi organization. The change to "German Youth group" did not change much until 1933. Our home evenings continued as usual, as did our journeys on holiday. We had to wear the black corduroy shorts and brown shirts with the "Sig-Rune" sown on the arm, as well as a black three cornered scarf with a leather knot. The only political action was the beginning of the glorification of Hitler. This was a procedure which affected the whole population, and progressed slowly until the seizing of power by Hitler.

From 30 January the situation in the country began to change. Not overnight, but slowly. The influence of the "National Socialist German Workers Party,"—the correct title, and not the generally accepted term "Nazi party"—progressed slowly. The political introduction for youth groups began in 1934, after I had decided to leave the group. There was a large influx of members at the end of January 1933, which meant that our group was too large, and must be subdivided into two further groups. I became the leader of these groups, and could be recognized by a cord which went from the left shoulder to the button-hole on the shirt pocket. Group leaders had a green-white cord, while the overall leader had a white cord. I became quite well known in the town, in a positive way.

The May 1, 1934, saw a big parade, in which the youth groups were allowed to participate. The new group, with drummers in front, was followed by the flag of the combined groups, followed in turn by the flags of the individual groups. It must have impressed the local inhabitants very much, but it was just a parade, with no political aims.

During the first months of 1934, I became leader of all the groups in the county. This allowed me to take part during the holidays in a leadership course, which took place in the castle at Hohenzollern. Afterwards my group activities came to an end, since I had left the youth movement. I was given, upon leaving, the permission to wear a white-red cord, until my joining the army. I also wore it during the final school exams.

5

THE SEIZING OF POWER, AND FINAL SCHOOL EXAMINATIONS

After passing the exams, the work began in earnest for the exams that had to be passed three years later. In history we dealt with the first world war and the period after. The Versailles Treaty was always a hotly discussed subject. The hard measures contained therein contributed to the economic crisis in Germany. People said it was a disgrace. A foreign minister, Mr. Stresemann, tried diplomatically to reduce the hardships. With the withdrawal of French and Belgian troops, along with the completion of the Dawes Plan in 1924 and the Locarno Pact in 1925, a certain relaxation was achieved. Many people saw that the conditions of the treaty could not be met because this would lead to the ruin of the country.

The increased economic problems resulted in several million people without work. They received no unemployment money or social help. This led to a depressive and unsatisfied public, particularly with the policies of the Weimar Republic, the government of the time. Political party disagreements without end brought the government much disrespect. The chancellor, Dr. Bruening, tried, with the aid of emergency powers in 1930, to get a grip on the economy. His policies led to an increase in the poverty of the people, while this caused deflation. The aim was to show the victors that it was impossible to continue with further reparations. This turned out to be the wrong policy, as the poor people became even poorer, which led to an increase in communist and national-socialist activities. The 30 Janurary 1933 saw the transfer of power to the National Socialists, under Hitler, by the German president Hindenburg. That evening, in every town a torchlight parade was held. In Geislingen a parade was held, organized by the S.A. (Sturmabteilungen) and the "Stahlhelm." This was an organization to which WWI front-line former soldiers belonged. Of course, we children, together with numerous bystanders, cheered from the sidelines. An over excited schoolboy even climbed the school flagpole and fixed a "Hakenkreuz" flag to it. When we arrived at school the next day, we found all the teachers, together with the school director, Dr. Werner, gathered by the flagpole. "Get that thing down" was their cry. None of the children volunteered to climb the flagpole, so the town's workers removed it.

Up to this time, most of the school faculty regarded the National Socialists with some reservation. Our English teacher was definitely against them. He was suspended at the end of 1933, after the responsible ministry in Stuttgart was filled with National Socialists. During 1934 we learned that two teachers had joined the NSDAP.

Until the end of my school days in March 1935, the political pressures were not too severe. Later, this was bound to increase with repression. One classmate joined the SA, while I remained in the youth movement.

There fell a dark shadow on the otherwise acceptable change of government. One day, my friend Ernst said he had something important to tell me. He was very distressed as he told me the following story. His mother re-married after his father, who was a captain, died during the war. What was not known was that his father was Jewish. Both Ernst and his brother were classed as "half Jews." Ernst had the same national feelings as us, and was also a member of our group. He was accepted as one of us. His antecedents were made known to all when, one day, written on the blackboard was "Ernst is a Jew." No-one knew who had written it. He took the final school exams with the rest of us, and was the best pupil. It was customary that the best pupil held the end of school speech. It was, therefore, a great shock for us as we were told that he could not make the speech because he was a "half Jew." This had been determined by the higher school authorities.

However, it did not prevent him from later joining the army for his duty period. After leaving, the father of a school friend arranged for him to attend a training course as a bank clerk at the Deutsche Bank. At the commencement of the war, he was conscripted into the army and took part in the invasion of France. During an action he distinguished himself and was awarded the Iron Cross, 2nd class, and was recommended for promotion. Then came from "higher up" the direction that instead of a promotion, he must leave the army. I can only say that it was stupid.

Ernst's younger brother was also in the army. I met him during a leave period. I found him highly decorated, and with the rank of sergeant. At the end of 1944, his unit in Norway gave the order from the gestapo in Berlin that he should be transferred there. The commander reported back that before the order could be carried out, he had been killed on duty. This was, of course, false. He survived the war, but was later killed in a road accident.

In 1944 Ernst was sent to an underground factory in Thueringen. His marriage was declared invalid by the authorities of the day. After 1945 it was legalized. During my time in Geislingen, I detected no political activity, either by the authorities or the "opposition." My parents sent me to the "peoples enemy," Dr. Kienle, for instruction in foreign languages. Although they belonged to the party, they maintained that such instruction had nothing to do with politics.

On my mother's side were several army officers. This influenced me in my decision to join a tank regiment that was stationed in Wuensdorf. In the summer of 1934 I was informed that I must report to the guardroom of the regiment. There I would take an entrance exam. I journeyed alone to Berlin. My godparent lived in a suburb of Berlin, so I visited her. I was introduced to her husband, and they both made sure that I arrived on time for the exam. Apart from me, there were another 30 applicants. A cousin of mine was adjutant of the regiment, and I rather expected to see him when I arrived. Instead, we were greeted by a staff-sergeant and taken to an arena, where we had to run some two miles, then high-jump and do other exercises. I did not have any problem with sports, so the testing was easy for me. Afterwards, three of us at a time were interviewed by a colonel Koreuber.

The first of us was asked what hobbies and interests he had. He answered literature, but he got somewhat confused when pertinent questions were asked. The second gave theatre visits as a hobby. He also was confused when questioned about particular shows. Colonel Koreuber had made notes, and gave these to an orderly with instructions which we could not hear. I answered that I was interested in motor cycle riding and the youth group activities. I was then asked to state on which side of the railway line from Stuttgart to Ulm the "Scharfenschlöss" lay. I answered, "Between the stations Suessen and Gingen, on the left." The colonel tried to persuade me that it lay on the right side. He showed me a map and asked me to show him where the castle was. This I did, apparently to his satisfaction. At that moment my cousin entered the room. He held a list of the theatre shows in Berlin. "Show the young man the mistakes he made about the shows he said he saw in Berlin," said the colonel. This was the first time that I saw my cousin. As we were requested to join the other candidates, he said to me that once the results of the exam were known, I would be collected by his men and taken to his home. As it turned out, I was one of three who passed the exam successfully, and so was accepted by the regiment, who only required 15 entrants for the year. My cousin, Heinz, told me that he had not shown himself during the day because he wanted to avoid showing any sort of favoritism. After we had eaten, he drove me back to my godparent's home. He was a rally-driver, and possesed many trophies, which he displayed in a cabinet. He raced for Hanomag, who had previously produced cars, as well as lorries. One of the cars was a 1.5 l sports car called "Sturm," in which Heinz won the Round Germany race in 1934. He showed his capabilites on the way to my godparent's house. We were driving at night on a straight road when we saw up ahead a level-crossing, which we were approaching at considerable speed. Suddenly, my cousin braked sharply and made a 180° turn. We ended up on the opposite side of the road. About 20 m behind us, a train crossed the road. The barriers were up. Heinz burst out of the car and ran to the control house. He came back a few minutes later and said that this time he would not report the man, as he had a family of six to support. We drove on to my godparent's home.

I decided that I must concentrate on the approaching final exams at school, since that would be my only chance to enter the army as an officer. I sold my motorbike, withdrew from youth groups, and began to "swot" for the exam. The results of the written exam were not divulged to us, but we had an idea as to the subjects of the oral exam. My weak points were math, physics, and Latin. The examiner said, after I had attempted to translate a Latin text, "It's a good thing you won't have to teach your soldiers Latin." As he said this a stone fell from my heart, as I realized I had passed, together with eight other classmates. I remember an occasion when our Latin teacher "flipped out" when I could not answer a particular question. He said, sarcastically, "Stupidity is God given, pray that you stay that way, otherwise you have nothing." In addition, he attempted to give me a slap, which I dodged, so that he slapped the wall behind me. His hand was bleeding and had to be bandged. He joined the Air Force, and we later met during a leave period, in Geislingen. He was honest with me and said, "I never thought that you would amount to anything. But now you are my superior officer." After this confession, we then had a drink.

Our end of school party was in my room at home, in which the youth groups had met previously. We had all drunk a bit too much, but decided to make our way to a place above the town which had a good view. On the way a few shop windows were demolished. This earned us a strong reprimand from the school director. We, naturally, paid for the damage, and apologized to the owners. In addition, we also threw empty wine bottles onto the railway line. The result was a fine from the local police for the whole class.

The class meeting at the end of March was the last time we met. The usual planned class meeting every five years could not take place due to the war, which broke out four years later.

I left home just before my 19th birthday at the end of March. Little did I know that there would be few opportunities for visits home, except for leave periods. It never occurred to me that in my generation the young years would be spent under war conditions, and afterwards, the difficult post-war period.

On my last evening at home, my mother came to me and gave me some good advice. I should treat all women with the same respect with which I treat my mother. Never play games where money is involved. Never visit casinos to play any of the games. For this advice I was thankful, and hope that I always held to it.

6

LIFE STARTS AS A SOLDIER

On 1 April 1935, I reported to the 3rd Prussian Transport Unit in Doeberitz-Elsgrund. I traveled with the night train to Berlin, then to Potsdam, and finally, after some 20 minutes walking, I reached the unit's guard room. I was wearing my youth-movement uniform, as I thought this would make a good impression. A guard took me to a barrack. I knocked on the door, and a voice said "Come in." I entered and said "Cadet Haeberlen reporting for duty." The barrack was furnished with two-tier beds, with two large and a small table. A man stood up and said that he was private Lang. I was asked if I had brought any money from home, to which I answered yes. "Good, you can go to the cantine and buy a crate of beer to celebrate your entrance." I laid my suitcase on the nearest table and went to the canteen. On my return, with a crate of beer, my suitcase was nowhere to be seen. I had, apparently, commited a big sin in that I had laid my case on the table, which was only for the use by the longest serving member of the barrack. While I had not requested with the words "Please may I have permission to enter," my suitcase was thrown out of the window, and I was given my first "telling-off." I retrieved my case and was shown to a bed. With me were also three other newcomers. We were then taken to a room where we received our uniforms and other items of clothing. Once more in the barrack, we four were sent to buy another crate of beer. After the evening meal and making our beds, we turned in. I will always remember that first night, as under my blanket I shed a lot of tears and asked myself why I had been so stupid as to join the army.

The shock in the morning at 5 o'clock, as whistles and loud voices awakened us and ordered us to "get up" is still with me. I was the first up, but my three comrades were a little slower and had to do 20 "knee-bends." They were told it should make them a little quicker the next morning. Since then, I have had no problem with waking up and being fully aware. On the morning parade, the sergeant informed everyone that there were four officer cadets, one of which was a "foreigner, " and that he was a Schwabe. Apart from me all the others came from Berlin or north Germany. This led to communication problems, due to the different dialects. I sometimes had difficulty in understanding what my comrades said, and they had difficulty understanding me. However, after a while the problem became less noticeable. The next day we were issued with weapons and our equipment was complete. We began basic training. Corporal Langesee was our instructor, and he was helped by a lance-corporal Fruhner, who was a family man with 7 years service. Promotion was not to be expected. There were many ranks with long service. A while later, due to Hitler's expansion of the army, things changed, and many were promoted. Almost on the same day as I joined, Hitler changed the army title from "Reichswehr" to "Die Wehrmacht." This included the navy and air force. Both the military training and the training on military transports, such as motorcycles, lorries, and cross-country vehicles was hard, but I learned how to deal with difficult situations.

Our instructor was strict, but fair. There was a high wall covered with rope netting on the parade ground. As a punishment one had to climb up and over this wall. After a couple of weeks, our instructor said that if one climbed over the wall in 30 seconds they were excused any futher climbing for that day. One Sunday a comrade practiced climbing this wall. We were shown a trick by the lance corporal whereby one could be quicker. The days training had just begun when our instructor became annoyed with me. "Haeberlen is grinning again," then came the order to climb over the wall. I did this in 30 seconds. Our instructor noted this, but said nothing. As the training was completed for the day, he asked me how I had achieved this time. Practice makes perfect, I answered, and explained that we had learned the trick of mastering the wall.

After the basic training, we were trained on the Pak 3.7 cm anti-tank weapon, then on an air-cooled MG 31. Maneuvering the Pak 3.7 on sandy ground was hard work, but we had to practice. Our driving instructor was a sergeant Moas. He said at the beginning of the instruction, "Haeberlen will teach us how to drive, he has a class 1 and 3 licence." We were first taught to ride a motorcycle. Eleven cadets were given a BMW 400. I was given a museum bike, a Victoria 600. This machine was so heavy that when it fell over I could not lift it upright again by myself. After a week's training we rode in convoy in a street with cobblestones, and it had been raining so the surface was wet. The instructor led the way in the control vehicle, the

BMW cadets came next, then me on my monster, and lastly came our instructor's helper. Suddenly, the bikes in front of me braked sharply. I also braked sharply, whereby I lost control of the bike, skidded, and ended up under a bus. I was lucky in that I only had abrasions, but the bike was damaged so that the steering forks were bent. This meant that I could not ride futher, so, after our instructor had arranged for the bike to be collected and delivered to a nearby garage for repairs, I traveled in the control car with the instructor back to our unit.

Two days later the monster was repaired and I took control of it again. After duty one evening, our instructor invited me to the canteen. This was unprecedented, as he had not attemped to make any social contact with us until now. He knew that the next morning we were going to be riding in rough land. He gave me a tip; when he passed me during the ride and raised his arm three times in the air, I should open up the throttle and go as fast as I could. This I did, and ended up in a rather wide and deep ditch! There was a loud noise, and it was found that the bike had broken forks and the rear wheel was broken out of its mounting. I lay in the ditch nearby, uninjured. Our chief instructor began to tell me off, but his assistant came to my rescue, and said that it was no fault of mine, as he had watched the way I had ridden. I was then given a BMW 400 like my comrades.

We then practiced very slow riding, whereby we had to come to a standstill without losing our balance, and I stalled the motor. Our instructor then removed the spark-plug and said I would have to push the bike the 30 km back to our unit. He then ordered the others to ride back. I remembered seeing a garage in a nearby village, so I pushed the bike there and bought a spark-plug, which I fitted in the bike. I then rode the rest of the way to within a couple of kilometers from our unit, where I rested in the grass for a couple of hours. I then rode to within a few hundred yards of the unit, dismounted, removed the plug, and pushed the bike the rest of the way. As I arrived at the motorcycle garage, our instructor wanted to know how I had returned in such a short time. I ran, was my answer. He felt the motor, but said nothing. I then cleaned, filled the bike, and parked it in its place in the garage. Next we had to learn to ride with a sidecar, and surprisingly, our instructor selected to ride in the sidecar with me riding the bike. A few weeks later, we entered the "Brandenburg Cross-country Examination," which included motorcycles, as well as cross-country vehicles. I was again surprised, as I learned that our instructor had selected me to ride with him. It was a 150 km ride. At 2 o'clock in the morning we started off, and if all went well, we would arrive just before lunch. We rode on a BMW 750. All went well until a few kilometers from our destination. As we rode through a big hole filled with water, the clutch gave up the ghost. We had a Bowden-cable as a spare with us, but the instructor said we should carry on without the clutch. We continued, but not for long, as we had to ride through a lot of sand. Of course, the engine stalled, so we had to change the Bowden-cable after all. This took some time, and we saw another contestant overtake us, which meant that we came in second. This took place at the end of September, and thereafter I was respected by the instructors.

During the summer we cadets were given a week's holiday. I naturally traveled to my home, in Geislingen, where I found that my grandmother was visiting us. My father had promised grandmother he would show her the plot of land and our week-end house on the Bodensee that he had bought. I was allowed to drive father's Mercedes 170. We stayed the night in a hotel in Hagnau, and the next morning we drove back to Geislingen. On the way, I did not feel too good. I soon developed a fever, and our family doctor found that my tonsils were swollen, and that I had a severe cold. He forbade me to return to my unit, and informed them that I would return later with the necessary doctor's certificate.

After 12 days I returned to my unit, only to find that new cadets were there. My unit had moved to Wuenstorf. I made my way to the railway station, and traveled via Berlin to Wuenstorf. I arrived at 10 o'clock in the evening. I found my instructor and gave him the doctor's note. He was very relieved to see me. The doctor's telegram had not arrived at the unit. He ordered me to report to the medical center straight away, which I did. Since in those days no antibiotics were available, I had to spend four days in quarantine to aviod infecting others. After the four days had passed, I was allowed to join my comrades. We spent the rest of the time in Zossen, in barracks.

Just after I had returned to my unit we were sent on maneuvers, which lasted 10 days. Most nights we slept in tents, but one night we slept in private quarters. There was a party held on the last evening, in Berlinchen, a small town which lay on a pretty lake. I was so tired that I returned to the hosts, who served me well.

We were hardly back in camp when we had to visit a marine unit in Kiel, where we inspected a U-boat. It was very impressive, but I could not imagine living under such close confines for long periods at sea. I was sure that I had chosen the right military branch. On the return journey we visited the hafen in Hamburg, and the Reeperbahn. At 1 o'clock in the morning we found our transport and traveled back.

Shortly before Christmas, we 12 cadets were promoted to corporal cadets. The promotion was made by our company commander personally. He often watched our progress, and gave us instruction in tactics. He was also present at the 10 day maneuvers.

On the evening of our "Passing Out" party, we wore our new uniforms with the shoulder "stripes" denoting our new rank. On the advice of the instructor, we had visited the tailors and were measured for our uniforms, which were finished in good time for the party. Our assistant instructor had also been promoted, so we celebrated well. We were looked on as representatives of the Unit when we were at the training school in Hannover, which we would attend in the new year. The morning after the party we were all feeling a little under the weather, but we all managed to travel our respective ways home on leave for Christmas and New Year.

7

ARMY WAR COLLEGE IN HANNOVER-LANGENHAGEN

At the end of training at the motorized school, I reported to the Army College in Hannover. The buildings were all new, and there was a large area for training purposes. Altogether, there were nine companies consisting of 200 cadets per company. Three cadets occupied a room. It contained three beds, three lockers, a large table, and three stools. On each floor was a washroom with showers and toilets.

With me in the room was a Waldemar Jung. He was a long serving active corporal with the horse-drawn artillery. Because of his good military service he was a candidate for promotion to officer rank. Franz was from the infantry and came from Bamberg. He, like me, had gone from school into the army. He was very reserved, but nonetheless a good comrade. Waldemar and I soon became friends, due to his open and friendly personality. We have, to this day, kept in contact with one another. After the time in Hannover was completed, contact was lost with Franz.

After five months of intensive training many were promoted to the rank of sergeant. From our company a few were sent back to their units, since in the view of the instructors they were unsuitable for officer training. They were mostly young men who could not cope with the strenuous training. As well as the theory training, we had sports training, including boxing. The sports instructor was not impressed with the behavior of a cadet named Haase. After a while, we became sparring partners. Our instructor asked who would fight with him. To our surprise, cadet Haase stepped forward. Our instructor was also surprised, and said, "Come and try your luck and show what you have learned." For the first couple of minutes Haase dodged the blows of our instructor. Suddenly, he threw a right hook which contacted, and the instructor was knocked out. After a few minutes he came round, and asked Haase where he had learned to box so well. Haase excused himself and said that he was the youth champion in middleweight boxing in Berlin. We did not have too many exercises in the practice area, while regular practice firing on the range was uppermost. Easter saw our company in the Harz mountains for skiing. In the summer we traveled to Kiel, where we visited a U-boat fleet, together with its supply ship. On the return journey we visited Munsterlager, where a demonstration of the latest tanks was taking place, including the first trial of the later well-known "Tiger" tank.

Our training included a visit to a dance school, which some 30 of us attended for instruction. There was no shortage of partners, as we were seen as suitable "objects" in the eyes of the young girls in Hannover. I had a problem just after the start of the lesson. During a social gathering it was customary, upon introduction, to kiss the ladie's hand, so one after the other we practiced kissing the hand of the teacher. I, however, objected to this, while after 29 comrades had "licked" her hand, I considered it unhygenic. I was naturally reported for this, and had to appear before the commander, General Lindemann. He wanted to know the reason for my refusal to kiss the lady's hand. I said, in my defense, that I would not refuse to kiss the hand of the general's wife, but kissing the hands of younger officer's ladies I would prefer not to do, since they were of the same age group as myself. I said I was against overdone etiquette, and preferred a more simple approach to people. Unexpectedly, the general said that while he did not agree with my views, he could accept other points of view. That was the end of the interview, and I could leave. Equally surprised was the company commander, who had expected the worst.

Over Whitsun we were given leave for a few days, and to my surprise my mother's brother, Erich, arrived in a smart American car—an Auburne sportscar—to collect me and drive me to Berlin. Erich, who was usually a film director active in America, was, at the moment, directing a film in Spain. The sportscar was used in the film, but he used it privately, as well.

The next day, at 6 o'clock in the morning, with me at the wheel, we drove from Berlin to Geislingen, to my parents, in a BMW cabriolet that my uncle had borrowed. We completed the journey in a record time of 10 hours, non-stop, bearing in mind that there were no motorways in those days. After the few days' leave, I returned to Hannover by train.

My comrade, Gerd Klinkicht, who was in the same group as me, came from Hannover and belonged to a canoe club that had a boathouse on the lake Maschsee. When I was at home during Whitsun, I heard from school friends that a second-hand folding boat was for sale. I went to look at it and bought it. From then on I spent many hours on the lake with club-members. Unfortunately, we lost contact with each other during the war.

During the previously mentioned dancing instruction, I had not found a suitable partner whom I could invite to our "Passing-Out" ball. I was, therefore, casting an eye out for a suitable partner. My comrade, Radzuweit, suggested that we go to the Geope. This was a dance-cafe with a 5 o'clock tea-dance. A small band played that was well known for its Tango music, as the band leader came from Argentina. We were both in uniform, which was, for me, unusual. We had just sat at a table which had an overview of the cafe, when I saw two girls. One was blond and attractive. It was not permitted to dance in uniform in this cafe. My comrade warned me as I stood up and requested a dance with her, and she told me that it was not allowed to be on the dance floor in uniform. I said that she appealed to me, and that I did not care. It was bound to happen, and on the dance floor I suddenly saw an officer from another company. We left the dance floor in a hurry. I escorted her to her table, and asked if my comrade and I might join them. They agreed, so we joined them. I then went to the table at which the officer sat and begged him not to report me, as I did not intend to dance anymore. Luckily, he turned a blind eye and said nothing.

Leni Diefenhardt was her name, and we met often. She also agreed to be my partner at the ball. On the following Sunday at 11 o'clock I was presented to her parents; otherwise, she would not have been given permission to attend the ball. As I approached her home, I noted that it was a large villa and assumed that her parents were well-off. Leni's father owned a machine factory. I was greeted in a friendly manner by her parents, who allowed Leni to attend the ball with me. Leni and her mother arrived at the ball in a chaffeur driven "Horch," a luxury car. As I escorted the ladies to our reserved table, I was surprised to find that my comrade, Radzuweit, was also present with Leni's friend from the Geope. Thereafter, we were often seen on Sundays together in my boat on the lake.

I remained in contact with Leni through letters after the end of the training at the army school. I visited her once or twice in Hannover, where the discussion centred around an engagement, whereby she would probably receive a BMW sportscar. We liked each other a lot, and were often together, but our relationship came to an end when I later met my first wife to be. In spite of this, I often thought of her.

Many years later, in 1974, we visited our daughter, Dagmar, in Hannover, where she lived at the time with her family. There I found Leni's telephone number. She was surprised to hear from me, and told me that she was still single and worked as a free designer in the textile branch, the same as me. We planned to meet, but this fell through as we left earlier than planned, and returned home. Radzuweit had married Leni's friend, but was killed during the war.

At the same time as we were promoted, we learned that to help the build-up of the air-force, 600 of us were required, preferably volunteers, to change to the air-force. I did not take much time to think it over. The next day I volunteered to remuster to the air-force. There were not so many volunteers, as many cadets stuck to tradition and stayed in the army, especially when relatives or fathers had served in the same unit. The air force was not held in high repute, which deterred quite a few from volunteering.

After Whitsun I reported to the medical unit of Goettingen University, where the pilot's entrance examination for the air force took place. This lasted two days. First, we were tested on a prototype centrifuge which went to 5 G, which is five times the pull of gravity. I had no problem with this, or with any of the psychological tests. I did, however, have a problem regarding the eye test. One of the checks involved looking into an instrument, into which little balls were fed. I had to say whether the balls fell in front of or behind a line in the instrument. My answer was not the one required. It meant that I had restricted night vision. A few choice words left my lips. The professor then asked if I was one of the volunteers who wished to join the air force. I said yes, and he then said he would turn a blind eye in this instance, but I must keep it to myself. So this was another test passed.

The officer's exams in Artillery, Tactics, Logistics, and War history began at the beginning of October. First came the written exam, then the oral exam. Also included was ability in sports. As in high school, I had difficulties with the theory, but nonetheless I succeeded in passing. The new uniform was ready a few days after the exams. I returned proudly to the 3rd Preussischen Vehicle Unit in Wuenstorf. I had an uneasy feeling regarding the reaction of my comrades because I had transferred to the air force. The unit commander had also transferred, so the disappointing remarks of my company commander carried no weight. Our previous instructor, Langesee, had, in the meantime, also been promoted. Both he and Fruhner, the other instructor, congratulated me, and we went out to celebrate. Our celebrations lasted the whole night. Langesee brought me to the train in the morning, and made sure I was seated for the journey home. I thanked him for everything, little knowing that we would meet again years later in Russia. During the journey I slowly became sober. In Geislingen, I enjoyed the admiring looks of the locals in my air force uniform. I was, however, excited by the thought that on 1 November I would be reporting to the airfield at Lagerlechfeld for training.

8

INTRODUCTION TO FLYING TRAINING IN LAGERLECHFELD

Before I went to my new unit I bought a car. It was a red two seater DKW open to all weathers, although a sail-cloth cover was available when it rained.

The engine was a two-cylinder, two stroke, which reached a speed of almost 60 mph. I drove to my new unit. There I had to report to the Fighterpilots School. I was very disapointed when I learned that I would be trained as an observer instead of a pilot. There were some 30 previous members of the Army-School, including Waldemar Jung, who had also volunteered for the air-force.

Lagerlechfeld was between Augsburg and Landsberg on the river Lech. It was known because of a battle which took place in August 955 AD. Otto the 1st won a battle against the Hungarians. The area was very flat, which was ideal for an airfield. Apart from us, there were other units under training. This meant that many diverse aircraft types were to be seen.

Apart from the practical flying duties, we were also trained in weather observation, which interested me. The instruction was given by meteorologists. What I learned stood me in good stead, later, during instrument flights. We also learned navigation, fighter tactics, all about various weapons and, of course, sport. The navigation instruction was given by retired sea captains with experience in passenger aircraft. Although all the instruction was indispensible, our greatest wish was to be able to fly. For most of us it would be the first flight ever.

Complete in flying suit, with helmet, goggles, gloves, and boots, and not forgetting a map of the local area, on 5 November 1938 I reported to Lieutenant Georg for my first flight. He was a rather small man, and he waited by a He 46 aircraft. This was a recconisance aircraft with one motor that was installed at the rear of the aircraft. It was an open two seater, with the pilot in front and the observer behind. There was also a mounting for a machine-gun, which was not fitted. Over the overalls a belt was worn. In the belt were two eyelets designed to accomodate the parachute that hung in the aircraft. To ensure that one would not fall out of the aircraft during flight, there was a belt fixed under the seat, the other end of which one connected to the belt with an eyelet. The lieutenant gave me instructions to follow the route on the map, and later tell him which route he had flown. A mechanic started the engine, the chocks were removed, and we rolled to the grass runway. As start permission was given with a flag and the throttle opened, I was pushed into my seat. After a short take-off, we lifted off. "Hurray," I shouted, "I'm flying." Suddenly, the pilot made a sharp climbing left turn. This pushed me to the right in my seat, so that I lost all sense of orientation. As we reached a height of about 1,200 ft. the flight turned into a nightmare. The pilot flew loops, steep turns, rolled a few times, then flew upside down. I was spared nothing. I did not know where up or down was, to say nothing of orientation with the map. We finally landed after 27 minutes, and I climbed out of my seat and stood uncertainly in front of the machine. "Well," said the lieutenant, "Still an enthusiastic volunteer for flying duties?" "Yes sir," I replied, but thought to myself, "You bastard!" as I made my way to my quarters. My comrades had had a more gentle introduction to flying on their first flight.

During the weeks until the end of the training, the time was divided between theory and flying instruction. Mostly, the flying instruction was given in the Do 23, while the navigation instruction was given in the Ju 52, an aircraft with three engines. This aircraft was also used as a passenger aircraft by the Lufthansa. It was also given in a Ju W 34, an improved version of the Ju W 33, in which the first crossing of the ocean from east to west was made by Hermann Koehl.

Fighter tactics were practised in the two seater He 45 and He 46. The Do 23 was a bomber with two engines. In the nose was room for the observer, who had a belt which prevented him from falling out of the aircraft. There was also a mounting for twin machine-guns. For target aiming, a somewhat primitive instrument was used which was situated on the floor of the fuselage at the rear. On target approach, we had to give the pilot hand signals. Because we flew at high levels, we wore a fur helmet and boots, together with a fur overall. Goggles and face protection were also provided. Compared with the present day, it seems rather adventurous.

The latest bomber often landed at Lagerlechfeld. This version was, of course, first delivered to operational units. Then we were given a delivery while we were still under training. This was in 1935. The old Do 11 and 23, with a couple of exceptions for training purposes, were withdrawn from service. They were completely overhauled, some even were given new engines. They were repainted, and carried Rumanian logos. We saw the transfer to the Rumanian air force first hand.

During our stay at Lechfeld, nothing spectacular happened. During the five and a half months I flew 59 flights, and knew the area from the air so well that I could fly from Augsburg to Landsberg and Ulm without consulting the map.

At the end of the training, and after passing the exams—both practical and theory—we were given a Certificate of Competance which showed that we had the ability to pilot an aircraft responsibly. We were also given a Certificate which showed that we could, as captain, fly an aircraft with a crew.

At the start of military flying, the training was carried out by privates, corporals, and sergeants. Officers with aircraft captaining abilities held mostly positions as squadron leaders. This changed during the following years, since the number of qualified aircraft captains had increased.

One day, Waldemar was with me in my DKW as I drove towards home for the weekend, and it was very cold so we wore our fur-lined flying suits. About 21:00 hrs we were somewhere between Ulm and Bergau, when in a curve I saw in the headlights a sheet of ice before us. It was too late to brake, and we spun around and hit the curb hard. Both the front and the rear wheels on one side were damaged, which meant that we could not drive any further. We pushed the car to a nearby farmhouse in which a light showed in one of the windows. We knocked heavily on the door until it was opened by the farmer.

We requested that we might leave the car in his yard until we had made arrangements for it to be collected and repaired by a garage, to which he agreed. We wrote our names on a piece of paper and gave it to him. We said that we would hitchhike to Augsburg. It was quite a while before a car came along that stopped on seeing our signs. The driver was a salesman who would be starting his tour in Augsburg. We were lucky to meet such a friendly man. He even drove us to the military airfield at Lechfeld, for which we were grateful. On the following Monday, I contacted my father and asked him to handle the collection and repair of my car. To this end he enlisted the help of a friend who was a director of a large weaving mill. He, in turn, directed his chauffeur to arrange things. As the chauffeur with a colleague arrived at the farm, they were immediately surrounded by police, who had the suspicion that they were spies. It turned out that the farmer had only seen us in our overalls. Our uniforms he could not see. He reasoned that we could have parachuted from an aircraft, and were agents. He made his way to the next village, which had a police station, and made his report. The police then started a search for two agents in the area.

The chauffeur explained the true position, and the search was called off. There came from "higher up" the request that things should be kept quiet, so that no one would be embarrassed. My car was repaired and delivered to my father.

At the end of our training, during the evening, we learned to which new unit we would belong. I was very pleased to find that I would join the 3rd Group of the Bomber Wing at Memmingen. This meant that I would be staying in south Germany, which, of course, pleased me.

9

III./GROUP BOMBER WING 255 MEMMIGEN

One day, after my 21st birthday, which was on 14 April, I drove via Landsberg to Mindelheim, a town with a ledgendary castle. Ledgend has it that an army captain, under the rule of Kaisers Maximilian the 1st and Karl the 5th, formed the local farmers into a disciplined fighting troop. My new unit in Memmingen lay on the main road. I could see it long before I arrived, from a hill which overlooked the town. The airfield had been recently built. It was about a mile and a half from the town, and was situated on higher ground. After I had reported at the guardroom, I was given an escort who came with me in the car, and directed me to the group commander, whose office was near the runway. Above the office was the control tower, and left and right were the hangars. I reported to the adjutant, a Lieutenant Maier, who was tall, thin, and had blue eyes. I was very impressed with him; he was the one I looked up to, until he was killed. After I had given him my papers, he questioned me briefly about my training, then led me through a door into the commandant's office, a lieutenant-colonel Mueller. He was of average height, with snow-white hair. On his uniform jacket he wore a medal from the first world war. Overall, he made a good impression on me. He also wanted to hear my previous history, then we shook hands and he wished me well, and hoped that I would soon adapt to my new life. An orderly was summoned who took me to 8 Squadron, to which I was attached. It was in the left hangar, in which the squadron leader also had his office. I introduced myself and found him to be an elderly Bayer, who seemed to be the fatherly type. "You will soon have enough of making reports," he said. "I'll get the sergeant to detail your batman, who will show you to your quarters, and in an hour's time we will meet in the Mess for a further chat." I had the feeling that I would get-along with him.

Airman Kutscher was the name of my batman. He showed me to my new quarters, which were on the ground floor. It had a living room, bedroom, and bathroom. Higher ranking officers lived on the floor above me. All rooms were furnished in the same way. My man was responsible for cleanliness and order in the flat. He was pleased to be with me and, until my transfer, remained by me. Today I see him every year at the annual reunion meeting of our Squadron.

I was satisfied with the situation of my flat. The single officer's quarters were at the west end of the airfield, and I was in the end house, which was near the officer's mess. Very practical. I met my squadron leader, as arranged, in the Mess. He wanted to know all about me, and mentioned that he was a flight observer who directed artillery during the first world war. He then informed me about everything I needed to know. There were two other young officers, Kurt Ziegler and Wilhelm Rath, who had arrived at the same time as me and were also attached to 8 Squadron. I met them in the Mess, together with three older officers. They were Lieutenant Jochen Poetter, Lieutenant Heino Wicke, the squadron technical officer, and Lieutenant Pavelcik, observer and navigation officer.

All newly arrived young officers at the squadron would be promoted to 2nd Lieutenant on Hitler's birthday. This gave us time to explore the surroundings, note where everything was, and generally find our way around. We had to report to the administration, and I was told that rent and catering in the Mess would be deducted from my pay. I received an additional flying allowance of 120 Reichmarks, but even so, there would not be a lot left over for personal requirements.

During the morning parade we were introduced to the "other ranks." The sergeants asked us if we would care to join them in the canteen to celebrate our arrival on the squadron, to which we gladly affirmed.

Most of the members of the squadron came from Schlesien, and during the evening I learned a few new words. One of these was "Koks." This was, naturally, a drink. First one chewed three coffee beans, then drank a "Schnaps," and finally a lump of sugar soaked in "Schnaps." After this liquid evening, my batman had difficulty waking me the next morning. Thereafter, both Kurt Ziegler and myself had a good understanding with the men responsible for the technical and armaments of the aircraft.

On 20 April we received from Lieutenant-Colonel Mueller our promotion papers. After a short speech, he requested us to adjourn to the mess, where a champagne breakfast had been arranged. Afterwards we drove into the mountains to

Oberjoch. We drove on a winding road that switched from Austria and back into Germany twice. We were proud to see that the customs men saluted us and allowed us to pass without any pass control. The evening found us in Memmingen, where we, on the recomendation of Captain Koegel, visited a wine tavern named Knoerringer. This became our favorite meeting place in the future. We went early to bed so that we would be fit to meet our new responsibilites in the morning.

Our duty was split between flying and navigation tuition, and also weapon training. We had to quickly learn all about the new bomber aircraft, the Do 17, with which the squadron was now equipped. The Do 17 had two in-line BMW engines. It carried a crew of three; pilot, observer, and radio-operator cum weapons operator. Since it had twin rudders and a thin fuselage, it soon earned the nickname "Flying pencil." At this time we were not permanently crewed. I flew with different members as pilots, such as private Schulz, lance-corporal Spanheimer, and corporals Sonntag, Sippel, and Mitschke, together with Lieutenants Wicke, Lange, and Schallenberg. I also flew with the deputy squadron leader, Lieutenant Poetter, who was also responsible for training the new lieutenants in flying. We made overland flights, bombing flights, blind flying using only the compass, and target practice using dummy bombs. Longer flights overland were also made to southern Germany, to Cottbus and Altenburg.

As my training was originally on motor transport, it was decided that I would be transport officer, a responsible position which gave me much pleasure. I was the only one with a driving license for all classes of transport, but extended the range to include a bus license. Without the help of sergeant Besendahl, I would not have achieved so much. He controlled the vehicle park and the workshop. I could always rely on him, although the final word was, naturally, with me. We had a very good working relationship.

Apart from the new Do17 the squadron also had an older Do X1, a Ju 52, two W 34s, and an Arado 66. These represented the classes A1, B1, B2, and C2. The aircraft were classified by the number of engines and weight. My greatest desire was to be a pilot, and I now had the opportunity. The commander allowed all trained observers to take pilot tuition, provided one could find a pilot to train them in their own time. Two pilots, one named Lieutenant Haenschen and the other named Piller, were prepared to teach me after duty hours. They both came from 9 Squadron. I reached the standard required for all classes of license by the end of the year 1938. The required overland flights I made during the weekends. One Saturday, with a colleague, I made the required night flying starts and landings. I was now qualified to fly all types of aircraft.

At the start of 1939 I was transferred to the Air War School in Werder. On the way I flew a Ju 52 around the countryside so that I would have the necessary flying hours required for the license.

I had very little free time, so I seldom visited the pretty town of Memmingen. I often traveled to my home in Geislingen to visit my parents, or when they were in Summer in Hagnau, I visited them on the Bodensee. I exchanged my small DKW car for a larger DKW, a four seater limousine with a special suspension system. As the officer in charge of transport, there was never any problem with repairs or servicing.

I will never forget an experience I had as a young lieutenant. A radio operator from another squdron was killed when his aircraft crashed. He came from a village in the Illertal valley. I was detailed to arrange the military funeral proceedings, with a guard of honor. We traveled in a lorry, and while the men sorted themselves out after we arrived, I met his parents and said my condolences. I then asked what the proceedure would be. The father informed me, then he said that he wanted to explain that his son volunteered for service in the air force against the wishes of the catholic priest. He did not want to hear anything against his son from the priest. He then requested my help in the matter.

I thought for a moment, then realized I was in a position to help this father. After the coffin with flowers, steel helmet, and radio-operators badge had arrived, the usual catholic ceremony began. This consisted of personal details and the life of the departed. The priest then started to say that he was against...He did not get any further, as I gave the order to the guard of honor to aim in the air and fire, fire, fire. I had managed to interrupt the priest's speech successfully. I then laid the wreath of the air force on the coffin and spoke the prepared words. The coffin was then lowered into the grave as the priest said a blessing. This was the end of the ceremony. I might add that I was given some very un-Christian looks from the priest.

As we prepared to leave in our transport, the father appeared and thanked me profusely. He then invited us to a Leichenschmaus. The hospitality was generous, to say the least, so much so that some of the guard of honor were "under the influence" when we arrived back at the squdron. Later, our squadron leader received a letter of thanks from the family, who were pleased that the priest was prevented from making his speech.

Until this time, I was without female company, not counting the ball which I attended with Leni. Then, on a swimming outing, I met a girl. I, together with my comrade, Kurt Ziegler, visited a nearby lake. As we were swimming, this girl sprang in the water, very close to me. Naturally, we came into conversation, and I learned that her name was Kaethe. We decided to return to Memmingen on our cycles. As we parted, I introduced myself, and we arranged to meet the following day, in the wine-tavern Knoerringer. It turned out that she was a clerk in the department for the German young Girls Association. We had straight away a common ground due to my activities in the Youth Organization. She lived in rented accommodations in Memmingen, but came from Erbach, on the river Neckar. We were soon good friends, and I invited her to the coming Mess Ball. I introduced her to my superior officer, as was the custom. He said she was a smart girl, which was his way of showing approval. In time I introduced Kaethe to my parents and, when on Sundays I was free from flying, we visited the Bodensee.

A special occurrence stands out in my mind. It was 15 March 1938, as we were flying a celebration flight over the Hohen-Tauern and the Grossglockner to Klagenfurt. The occasion was the rejoining of Austria with Germany. This is now refered to as the "occupation" of Austria, which is completely wrong. The enthusiasum with which the German army was greeted tells another story.

To prepare for a fly-past at the "Reichsparteitag" to be held in Nuernberg, we were moved to an airfield at Gelnhausen, for practice. I have no happy memories of that airfield.

In May 1938 we flew in Spessart for bombing and firing practice. I was observer in the aircraft piloted by Heino Wicke. After take-off, he flew a low circle around the town of Memmingen, where his fiancé lived. The next day, 5 May 1938, we practiced single engine flying. I was given special orders from the squadron leader, which meant that Heino Wicke must have another observer. I had completed the task set by the squadron leader and sat next to him in a chair by the barracks, watching the aircraft. Heino's aircraft was at a height of about 6,000 ft, and we could see that he was flying on one engine. Suddenly, the aircraft side-slipped and plunged vertically. The engine howled loudly until the aircraft hit the ground. We jumped into the duty wagon and went as fast as possible to the crash site. It was a terrible sight. The Do 17 had crashed into a stream, from which only the wings were visible, while the rest lay embedded deep in the muddy waters of the stream. We found nearby, not only the cabin roof, but the top of the pilot's head, which showed that he had attemped to leave the aircraft. This was the first time that I experienced the death of a comrade first hand.

I was given the unpleasant task of informing his fiancé and her family, since I was often with them in the wine tavern. To this end I flew straight to Memmingen. When I had this difficult task behind me, I was ordered to attend the funeral in his home town. We flew three Do 17s to Goerlitz, and then with transport to the family's home. I said my condolences, together with those of the squadron leader and the group commander. I would take part in the burial ceremony. His mother expressed the desire to see her son in the coffin, before he was finally buried. I took the father to one side and, with a lot of skill, explained to him that there was not a lot of Heino in the coffin. It sounds strange, but the two low fly-pasts we made at the end of the ceremony ended the weeping of the participants. The parents requested me to thank my comrades for the fly-past. They felt that this was in accordance with their son's wishes, as flying was his life.

Jochen Poetter, a comrade, had better luck. He had been detailed to fly an instrument flight practice in a Ju 52 to Hamburg and back. He had a crew of six, and was due to return in the evening. As it was a Friday, all officers had assembled in the mess for the usual beer evening. The commander decided to wait with the meal until he heard the Ju 52 fly over, which meant that the landing would follow shortly. An orderly reported to the commander that the Ju 52 was in the area. He ordered the meal to begin, as Jochen Poetter would soon arrive. Time passed, but no Jochen Poetter arrived. The commander then went to the telephone. He came back and informed us, with a very white face, "He has not landed, and there is no trace of the aircraft." We were stunned, and we sat there as if carved from stone. No one could eat anything, let alone drink. Now I knew what "crash feeling" was, over which we often joked. After about one and a half hours, there arrived suddenly a vehicle at the mess, and out got Jochen Poetter, somewhat the worse for wear, but unhurt. He reported to the commander, "4 miles from the runway, on approach we made an emergency landing. Crew unhurt, but aircraft a complete write-off." We were all naturally agog to know what had happened. In the clouds Poetter had received the order, via radio, to overfly the airfield. As it was a blind flying exercise, he ordered the crew to make a blind landing. Everyone knew the drill and acted accordingly.

As Poetter came through a break in the clouds and saw the lights of the airfield, he took over the controls with the words, "I will land the aircraft, as I am expected in the mess." He then made a low turn, but a wing brushed a hillside which was nearby. The wing was ripped off, and this caused the aircraft to crash. The Ju 52, luckily, first hit the ground with the landing gear, which was torn off. The engines also broke away, and the fuselage came to rest in a field some 100 ft. from a wood. We were all relieved that no one was injured. We never found out what the commander and Poetter said to each other, but he suffered no adverse reaction

Shortly afterwards, Lieutenant-Colonel Mueller was transferred to Muenchen, and we were given a new commander. He was Lieutenant-Colonel Alois Stoeckel, a Bayer from the backwoods, but he was on the ball and had, at the same time, a friendly disposition. He was soon respected by all ranks.

I was ordered to him in the middle of December 1938. Without any idea why, I reported as ordered. I was as if struck by lightning as he said that he had received an order to send a suitable officer as an instructor for the Air War School in Werder. He had selected me! A lieutenant-colonel from Werder had telephoned and said that he did not want any lieutenants from the 850 officers with rank number 801 as an instructor. Our commander had answered to the effect that as commander of the 3rd Group 255, he had selected lieutenant Haeberlen, based on his judgement, as suitable for the post, and would accept no remarks as above. "If you like, I will accompany you to Werder if you don't trust yourself alone to beard the lion in his den." I said that this would not be necessary. In parting, he said that such a post lasted 18 months, thereafter he would request that I return to him so that we could continue to work together.

I had only been in Werder a few days when he arrived in a He 111. He asked me if there were any problems. He spent some time with the training commander under whom I served, then returned to me. We went to his aircraft, where he said, "Don't disappoint me, or I will never look at you again." We shook hands, and he climbed into his aircraft and flew back to Memmingen. I do not think I disappointed him. After 18 months I returned to Memmingen, where the group was in action against France and England. He failed to return after an attack on England as the squadron leader.

I recall an incident that shows the simple and direct manner with which he carried out his duties. A new doctor was assigned to the group, and in accordance with custom, he wore his best uniform and, with his wife wearing an elegant costume, presented themselves on Sunday to the commander and his wife. The commander lived in a house which lay between the airfield and Memmingen. In the drive was an old DKW with the bonnet up, and from under the car protruded a pair of legs. The doctor, with his foot, shook the protuding legs and asked if the commander lived here. The legs answered "Of course." The doctor then asked if the commander was at home. The commander then appeared from under the car and said, "Yes, I am at home. You look a bit surprised." He then invited the pair into the house. He was an excellent commander, and an unusual man.

In October 1938, a sergeant, private, and I were seconded for a special duty. We were given a motorcycle with a sidecar, with which we would drive to Breisach on the Rhine. There we reported to the border control west. For 14 days, in eight hour shifts, we had to observe, from a concealed part of the town wall, the opposite side of the Rhine, which was French. We had to note all military vehicle movements, together with any bunker construction for the French army. We lived in a nearby pub where we were treated in a motherly fashion by the landlady. Apart from French reconnaissance aircraft, there was nothing special to report. It was almost like two weeks leave, since we had good weather for the whole period.

I became close friends with several comrades, including Haenschen Lange, Kurt Ziegler, Teddy Schwegler, and Wilheim Rath. They came with me, in rotation, when I traveled home on free weekends. Haenschen and my sister, Hanna, soon became very good friends. The friendship did not last very long, though. Later she became very friendly with Kurt, which led to them eventually getting married. Kurt started in a W 34 from Stetten, but crashed when the engine failed. His left leg had to be amputated. He then completed an engineer's course, which meant that he had better expections of a position. He was also of an inventive nature; by playing around with mechanical problems, he often came up with amazing results. After the war his marriage failed, mainly due to greater interest in his work than in his family.

Haenschen was killed during an attack on the Russian island Krim. He is buried in Bakschiseraja, which is next to the well-known monastery. Wilhelm was shot down in an attack over Plymouth, and Teddy was killed a few days before the end of the war, in Ansbach. Only the day before, I had spoken with him on the telephone and warned him. I tried to explain to him that the war was lost, and he should concentrate on his family and not on fighting.

Apart from Bayern the rest of Germany had been over-run, and it was pointless to fight further. Unfortunately, until the end of the war, he was not the only one who did not listen to me.

10

AIR WAR INSTRUCTING IN WERDER

At the beginning of 1939 I took leave of Kaethe, my comrades in the mess, and the sergeants and corporals in the cantine. I took farewell of the squadron leader and the commander, and flew, with my baggage, back to Memmingen in a Ju 52 accompanied by Teddy Schwegler, who was to fly the aircraft. I made a sweeping curve over Memmingen as a farewell gesture, and saw the snow covered high Allgaeus in the distance. I flew with a heavy heart to my new post in Werder. As I still wanted some flying hours to complete the C-2 flying license, we flew east-wards until shortly before Prag, then northwards to the the coast of the Baltic sea, and then set course for our destination, Werder. On approach the view was quite pleasant. The airfield lay on the edge of town and was bordered in the north by the river Havel, which at this point was quite broad. The view lifted my depression somewhat. After reporting to the adjutant I was given a course to train soldiers to enable them to sit for the officer's exam. Teddy helped me to move in to my new quarter, then flew back to Memmingen. As it was now lunch time I found my way to the officer's mess, and on the way I met a lieutenant-colonel whom I saluted. He had red shoulder tabs, so I deduced that he was an artillery man. He asked me if I was new here, to which I replied yes. "And how do you like your new post?" he asked. I answered to the effect that it was the worst possible thing that could have happened to me. "I think you will soon adapt to here, and that it will not be too bad." We entered the mess foyer where some officers were sitting, waiting for the meal to begin. They sprang to attention, and I knew that the lieutenant-colonel by my side was the commander of the training school. I could not imagine that an artillery officer was the C.O. I had assumed that a pilot with yellow tabs would be the C.O. "What have you to say now?" he asked me. "Nothing," was my laconic reply. It soon became obvious that he did not hold my remarks as anything serious, and there was soon a good understanding between us.

The school had two separate arms; one was for cadet corporals who wished to take the officer's exam, and the other was for cadets who came from basic training. They were given training on aircraft up to B 2 level. I now had an aim, which was to change to a course in which aircraft captains were trained. I did not tell anyone of my plans, but made contact with instructors who could possibly be of help to my plans.

I was given a class of 32 new arrivals on 1 February. They were all high-school "leavers" who had been trained in various army branches. Some were my age, or a couple of years younger. It was clear to me that I would not have an easy time as instructor with this class. Most of the training was given by the older and more experienced officers. I gave instruction on the firing-range, sport, and "Behavior in Company." To this latter end I drove with the class to Potsdam, where once a week a dancing hour had been arranged. This was great fun for the trainees, but not so much fun for me. There was no shortage of eligible young girls, who were on the lookout for a would-be officer. Trouble was, that many of the girls' mothers also attended the dance hour, to keep an eye on their daughters, which meant that I spent most of the time, uncomfortably, in their company. It was most difficult to talk my way out of the many invitations I was given. When I said I was engaged it did not seem to make any difference.

During the Easter holiday Kaethe and I became engaged in Geislingen. She had left home because her father, as mayor of Erbach, on the river Neckar, had indulged in dubious activities which led to his arrest by the police, and an eventual prison sentence. That Kaethe had deserted her mother at such a time was beyond the understanding of my mother, who advised me against the engagement. Nontheless, the official engagement party was held in our house, attended only by members of my family, together with my comrades Schwegler, Rath, Lange, and Ziegler.

My class was always on the lookout for an opportunity to put one over on the instructor. The firing range lay some one and a half miles from the school, and after we left the guard-room we passed through a village. I gave the order "Sing." This they did, but it was an indecent song, so I ordered "Stop singing." After a while I again ordered "Sing, but another song." With large grins on their faces they started to sing the same indecent song. "Stop singing," I ordered. The range was in a clearing in the middle of a wood, and as the road lay in the near from the runway, we were constantly overflown by training aircraft. I gave the order that until we reached the range, whenever an aircraft flew over, they would take cover in the wood as if it were an air attack. The continuous jumping for shelter under trees, then reforming, had its effect. After half an hour they were all in. After the firing practice, we marched back to the school. On the way I gave the order "Sing." Of course, they began the same indecent song, so I gave the order "Stop singing." Before I dismissed them in the school, I said to them, "Gentlemen, you have two possibilities; either you work with me, or you work against me. You have the choice, but think very carefully before you decide which is best for you and your careers." I then dismissed them. They never tried to put one over me again.

In sport I preferred light athletics, but I also found pleasure in handball and swimming. I entered a 100 m race against the five fastest cadets and won. Today, one would say that my image had improved. In handball, because I was quick, I had the right flank position in the team of the Geislingen sports club. During the county championship games, I was rammed so hard by an opponent that I was unconsious for a few minutes. This led to my parents forbidding me to play in games where points were scored. I was in the Geislingen swimming club, and I practiced a lot. My speciality was diving from the 10 ft diving board. I also did a lot of diving in the school's swimming pool. I also swam 50 m under water, a personal record. This was only eclipsed by a cadet who swam 60 m under water.

I demonstrated the backwards spring from the 10 ft diving board into the pool for the class. I then said that they should all follow my example. Most did, but there were a few who could not pluck up enough courage to spring. Only my threat that if they did not spring, they would not be allowed to take the final exam, had its effect. The rest sprang.

Learning correct behavior in society was also included in the instruction. This I combined with practical demonstrations, whereby the cadets would act out the roll of, for instance, the parents of a daughter who wished to be invited to the "Passing-out" ball by a cadet. Then, the arrival of the cadet at the home between 11 and 12 o'clock, complete with a boquet of flowers for the mother. This and other similar situations where etiquette had to be observed had to be learned by the cadets. Also, conversation and manners were also taught, together with correct dress.

I was ordered by the commander, along with other officers, to attend the Garrison-Ball in Potsdam. This presented me with a problem, in that I did not posses the appropriate dress uniform. Previously, in Memmingen, the commander had said to me that I need not buy the expensive uniform, and in the meantime it was forgotten. I reported to my superior officer, a Captain, and informed him that I did not posses the correct uniform. He ordered me to purchase one straight away. In answer to my question as to whether the normal uniform was acceptable, he reported me to the

Commander of the school. As I stood before him he asked if I had money problems, to which I answered in the negative. "Evidence?" he asked. I said, "My savings book," and laid it on the table. He saw that I had saved over 1,000 Reichsmarks. He then ordered me to buy a dress uniform.

To this effect I drove to Potsdam on a Saturday to a uniform tailor. I explained to him that I was an instructor at the school, and that my cadet class would soon be sitting the final exams, and would then require new uniforms. I then asked for a rebate, and mentioned that I would need a made to measure dress uniform with all the trimmings. The tailor was beside himself with the thought of such a large order. I told him that I would bring him a list with the names of the cadets who would be requiring uniforms on the following Saturday. My cadets had been shopping around to inquire about the cost of a uniform, and when they heard the price my tailor would charge, 25 of them said that yes, that would suit their pocket. As arranged, I gave the tailor a list of names of the cadets who would buy their uniforms from him. The tailor said it was an honor to serve me, and he would measure me for my dress uniform, which would be ready in plenty of time for the Ball. That was my first financial contact with the commercial world.

The forthcomming Ball filled me with some trepidation, and no doubt the other officers, as well. Not only did we have to wear the dress uniform, but white gloves, as well. The evening finally arrived, and we duly appeared together in the ballroom. The commander of the regiment, the 9th Infantry Regiment Potsdam, led us to our female companions, who were seated at a table. This regiment was the most traditional in north Germany. Our companions were attractive girls, and we danced the first obligitary dance with them, of course, wearing the white gloves. After the first dances, our air-tactics officer, Major Schroeder, made his way unnoticed to the dance band leader and requested a "Cha cha cha" dance. The impossible happened in such elegant company. Younger officers started to dance to the latest dance rhythm, and the whole atmosphere changed. I was the first to remove my white gloves, and others followed suit. We were given frowns and raised eyebrows from the more conservative older officers, but there was still a change from a stiff formal occassion to a more enjoyable occassion. We danced until one o'clock in the morning, and it pleased our major that he had broken through the strict social barriers.

In our barracks, we felt the wind of change in the political scene. The government heads from England, France, and Italy were in Muenchen to discuss with Hitler the separation of the German Sudetenland from Czechoslovakia. The tension was reduced a little with regard to the foreign policies. No one, either us or our families, concerned ourselves with the thought of war. Hitler, and Goebbels, had so often repeated that their policies were of a peaceful nature, and that the government's demands would be achieved through discussion. Today's generation cannot understand the strong wish of the people with regard to the return of lands given away at the end of the first world war. It was even preached in the schools that this was a German right. It was in the late summer that Polish saboteurs were active on the German Polish border, but even then, there was no special military action that we could detect.

The course that started in February ended in August. The cadets had to pass exams, both written and oral, in the separate subjects they had learned. Afterwards, they were given the results, and learned whether they were now potential officers or not. On 1 September, the promotion party took place for the cadets who had passed the exams. It was an amazing coincidence that on this day Hitler, who had promoted himself to army chief, gave the order to attack Poland. This decision came as a surprise to all, as it was so unexpected. We all thought that it would not last long, and saw the future optimistically. This was strengthend by the news of the rapid advance of the German troops.

When I think back on those days, I can remember the young men, full of confidence, with only one thought in mind; travel quickly to their unit, and enter the war. This made me sad, as only a few of them ever returned. One or two I met during the war. One was Hogeweg, who was stationed in Poltawa, in southern Russia. He was the commander of a fighter squadron, and my group was stationed there for a while. After the war, I met, quite by accident, another comrade, Hermichen, who was the commander of a fighter squadron during the war. He also was decorated with the knights cross. He held the position of personnel director for Karstadt, a supermarket chain. He had helped many of his ex-comrades find jobs. As we met, his first question was could he do anything for me. I did not need any help, thank God, and answered his friendly question in the negative.

During my time as instructor in Werder, I got to know the chief instructor responsible for training aircraft captains, named Captain Bischof. We had a common love of tennis, which brought us nearer. With his help I was able to become familiar flying various types of aircraft. Weekends I flew to Friedrichshafen to be with my family on the Bodensee. Sometimes I flew to Goeppingen, which was near my home town. One day in the mess, he asked me if I could fly multi-engined aircraft. I answered yes, I could, and was given the task to test fly, with a technical engineer, a Do 17 that was newly repaired.

I had flown considerably in a Do 17 as observer, but had not sat in the left hand seat. As we stood in front of the aircraft, I had to muster up the courage to fly the machine without making any mistakes. Starting was no problem, but the thought of landing filled me with some doubts. The first landing with an unfamiliar aircraft is always difficult, but luckily, all went well. The test flight required that a height of some 13,000 ft be reached before the various required maneuvers were executed. This was all carried out successfully, and after the flight I explained to the technician that it had been my first flight as captain of a Do 17. He remarked, "Lieutenant, you can captain all the coming test-flights, since the flight was without failure." I asked him if he would be so kind as to repeat that to senior-lieutenant Thomas.

Shortly after my cadets had successfuly passed their exams, and received their promotion, Captain Bischof asked me if I was satisfied with my transfer as instructor for aircraft captain's training courses, since for the next course an instructor had failed to report. I had to burn the midnight oil to learn myself all the flight theory and everything that I would later teach the students. I did not see any problems, but I was glad that I had told no one how I had achieved my flying license. On 1 October I was promoted to Lieutenant. In peacetime such promotions took longer, but due to the war the period was shortened. One advantage of the promotion was that my purse became heavier. After the successful completion by my pupils for the aircraft captain's flying license exams, and during the inevitable party, I confessed to Bischof that I had never attended an aircraft captain's school. He, and the other instructors, found this hard to believe.

One of my students, Hans-Joachim Marseille, later was highly decorated, and well known. He wore the Knights-cross, with Oak Leaf and Diamond. As pupil and soldier, he was always the easy-going type. Once, he failed to return after an overland flight, but telephoned from a police station in the countryside by Brandenburg. He reported an emergency landing in a field due to engine failure. Technicians from a nearby airfield, called in to make repairs, reported that they could find no engine fault, apart from a closed air-flap on the carburetor. This could cause intermittent ignition, which affected engine performance. The next day he took-off from the field and returned to base. In the Spring of 1941, we met again. He was now a highly decorated Captain. He laughingly admitted that the engine failure was faked so that he could impress his then girlfriend with a landing. Her parents owned a large amount of land, in a field of which he landed. I then told him that in my final assessment of him, I had recommended that he be further trained as a fighter, and not as a bomber pilot. It would appear that I made the correct decision, for by then he was one of the best fighter pilots, especially in dog fights. His grave is somewhere in North Africa. He died, not due to enemy action, but to the engine failure of his Me 109, which caused him to leave the aircraft. In doing so, he got caught on the tail of the aircraft and sustained a broken back.

In Werder, two years later, I met a former pupil who had transformed from a frivolous schoolboy to a serious minded Captain. Quite a few of my previous pupils showed outstanding ability during the war. Unfortunately, few of them survived, as many died while in Russian captivity.

After the occupation of Poland, the political situation changed dramatically. England and France had declared war on Germany, and Hitler and the Russian dictator Stalin were discussing the division of Poland between them. Neither of the dictators had a permanent desire for co-existence. The Hitler/Stalin pact had been handled by Molotov and Ribbentrop, who was deputy for von Weizsaecker.

Von Weizsaecker was the father of our future Bundes-President. He was a previous member of the Potsdam 9th Infantry Regiment. Often in his speeches, particularly when abroad, he referred to the war in an, for us old soldiers, enigmatic manner. He gave the Germans a historical fault that was not correct, and this view is held by many who lived at the time and were involved in the war. Even members of the Allied Forces knew the difference between fair fighting soldiers and the actions of the SD, who did not recognize the normal command structure. For this reason von Weizaecker is, for us, a traitor to his previous comrades.

Due to the strained situation, many who were engaged took advantage of the short leave periods to get married. With Kaethe and me it was difficult to fix a time, but we finally got married in October, in Geislingen. The party was held at my parent's house, again without Kaethe's family. As well as my brother and sisters, a few comrades from Memmingen turned up. We spent our honeymoon at the hotel "Traifelberg," at the edge of the Schwaebischen Alb, higher up than the well-known Lichtenstein castle. The hotel was situated in a woodland area, and as we were both nature lovers, we enjoyed a short honeymoon with agreeable Autumn weather. Then it was back to duty.

In January 1940 I managed to obtain a flat in Babelsberg-Ufastadt. It was complete with all the furniture, including bedding and everything necessary in the kitchen. The landlady was a friendly elderly widow. I let Kaethe know straight away of our luck. Her reaction hit me like a blow from a hammer. I had expected that she would pack her suitcase, give up her job, and join me, but she had other plans. She said that she would be away skiing in the Allgaeu for a week. I thought this was a little unfair, as we were living in wartime and now had the opportunity to live together. For how long, one could not tell. At the moment it was in order, so long as I retained my post at the school. The fact that she did not join me straight away hurt, although I did not admit this to myself at the time. She joined me after her ski holiday, and we enjoyed many happy moments together. I traveled to Werder and back every day with the tram. This meant that we had to get up very early every morning, as my work commenced at 7 o'clock, sometimes earlier. I was glad, therefore, that I had retained my accommodation in the barracks, where I could spend the night when late flying or exercises were being held, and I could not get home. I had at least expected to remain at Werder until the present training course ended, but this was not to be. It came as a surprise that I was to be transferred. As Kaethe knew no one in Berlin, she returned to Memmingen, where we moved into newly built officers' quarters, close to the airfield.

11

TEMPORARY TRANSFER TO 4 SQUADRON BOMBER WING FOR SPECIAL TASKS

I could not explain my unexpected transfer to a transport squadron, stationed in Braunschweig, until my interview with the Commander. I then learned that I was to attend a course as dispatcher in a parachute school. I further learned that in the near future the invasion of England was being considered, and this was the reason for my transfer. Again, my hopes of an aircraft captain's position were dashed. So began the jumping practice for the parachutists. My job was to see that when we reached the jumping zone the waiting parachutists jumped. Occassionly, I had to gently push a reluctant jumper out of the aircraft, which was a Ju 52. I also had to see that everything proceeded quickly. I often had the opportunity to fly the Ju 52 to pick up supplies for the school and our Group. I flew in a northerly direction between Braunschweig, Stargard, Tutow, and Jueterbog. The aircraft was often filled to the top of the fuselage with parachutes and other things which we required. During these flights, I gained much experience in flying in bad weather conditions. At the end of the training, I had to report to the Group's adjutant, whereby I was naturally curious as to the reason. He informed me that the Commander of my previous Squadron had requested my return. The unit's title had changed. It was now the 3rd Bomber Group 51. They were now stationed in Etampes in France. To say that I was pleased was an understatement. The next day, 7 October 1940, I flew, accompanied by my comrade Grosse, in a Ju 52 to my new unit in Etampes, France.

12

RETURN TO MY UNIT IN FRANCE

The group 104 Stargard-Etampes for special tasks, to which Wing I belonged, was now in France. There had been some changes made. The Alpen 255 had been renamed Bomber Wing 51 "Edelweiss." Previously, every group had its motif painted on their aircraft. Group 1, for instance, had "Alpenveilchen," Group 2 had "Enzian," and Group 3 had "Edelweiss." This was the insignia now carried by all squadron aircraft. Headquarters and the 1st Group were stationed in Villacouble, the 2md Group were stationed in Villaroche, and the 3rd Group, to which I belonged, were stationed in Etampes, some 30 miles south of Paris. Shortly before Stargard, we made two landings to allow the passengers to depart the aircraft. Because the weather was so bad we had to fly blind, all the way to the airfield. Naturally, we did not get even a glimpse of Paris. I was excited about how I would find the group. How many comrades were still there, from the 8th and other squadrons? Who was now the Commander? As we approached the airfield, we saw that a part of a hangar had been hit by bombs. The airfield was constantly attacked during the offensive against France. The new Ju 88 A3 was the latest addition to the squadron. The aircraft stood a little apart from the hangar, near the runway. They were not even camouflaged, which seemed to suggest that enemy action was not expected.

As we parked in the visiting aircraft slot, I was able to see the activity going on by the Ju 88s. Technicians and armorers were working feverishly to prepare the aircraft for action. I telephoned headquarters from the dispersal, and was pleased to hear the voice of Lieutenant Bretschneider, whom I knew from Memmingen. He sent transport straight away, and our meeting was very cordial. As there was an air attack against England planned for the coming night, most officers were in the mess. I was informed by Bretschneider that Major Marienfeld was to be the wing commander, with squadron commanders Brand, Poetter, and Kind. This last name I did not know. With excitement, I entered the mess. I was first seen by Teddy Schwegler, who greeted me with enthusiasm, as did all those who knew me, including Wilhelm Rath, Peter Brand, Haenschen Lange, Fritz Kuechle, and Gerd Mueller. Teddy brought me to the Commander, whom I thanked for requesting my return. Marienfeld was an elderly man, small in stature, but built like a bull, with fading blond hair. He took me to one side, and wanted to hear all about my time at the war college, and my activities with the special tasks unit. Afterwards, he told me that I would be assuming the position of his adjutant. I would take over from Lieutenant Bretschneider, but until such time, I would rejoin the 8th squadron, where I would hold the position of aircraft observer. Due to his way of speaking, he was given the nickname "Loudmouth" He was a Lufthansa pilot before he transferred to the Air Force, and had much more flying experience than we "Youngsters," as he called us, had. In the beginning, we had a few differences of opinion, but later we understood each other very well. I attended the briefing for the night's attack on London, to orient myself as to how things were organized. From the tower I watched the aircraft take off every two minutes. This was because night attacks were made by single aircraft. Take-off time was approximately 23:00 hours, with London as the target. After about two to three hours the aircraft would start the return journey. Over England lay a weather depression, so that little flack and no night fighters were encountered, and all aircraft returned to base. After the long flight here, together with the new imprq"sions that I had received, I was exhausted, and as is so often the case, I found it difficult to sleep that first night in my old unit.

The first air attack on military seaports and "Royal Air Force" airfields was accompanied by heavy losses. An order that no bombs were to be dropped on civilian targets was disastrous. When the actual target was not seen due to bad weather, bombs were dropped too late. The result was that the aircraft were an easy target for the enemy fighters. Many crews who missing had to try to survive in the English Channel. Many aircraft were shot down during the return flight, and most of the crews perished by drowning.

On 25 April 1940 British bombers had bombed the holiday resort of Wenningstedt on Sylt, and the small town Heide in Holstein. In the report of the army Chief of Staff, it was stated "The enemy has extended the air war against undefended targets which have no military significance." This report, dated the day of the attack, is accepted by all serious students of history. Compare this with the report, from the same source, dated the 18 May 1940. Enemy air attacks on civilian towns, such as Hamburg and Bremen in North Germany, and towns in West Germany. On all these, and previous, occassions, except for an attack on some barracks, all were without military significance. So determined the German Chief of Staff. (A.a.O., S. 148). On 8 September 1940 the same source announced "The attacks by our air force on 6-7 September against military targets near London was continued on the 7th and 8th with heavily armed aircraft. This was the revenge for the continued, and heightened, attacks on non-military targets in Germany by the British air force." (A.a.O., S. 264). These attacks led to the withdrawal of the order that only military targets be bombed. It is not true what the enemy propaganda, and today's media, say, that the German air force started the terror bombing. This terror bombing was started by the British. Incidentally, the Anglo-American art to spread false information is far superior to anything we have. Sadly enough, the German media and history researchers seem to accept these lies. They, of course, know better. During the later war years, these terror attacks increased a thousand-fold, including, for instance, Dresden, Hamburg, Cologne, Stuttgart, Freiburg, Bremen, Pforzheim, Heilbron, Koenigsberg, Hildesheim, Wuerzburg, Nuernberg, Bruchsal, and the list continues. Enough said.

The next morning, I was detailed by Squadron-Leader Poetter to join the crew of Teddy Schwegler as observer. As I made my way to the runway and the Ju 88 I met, first of all, the chief technical Flight Sergeant, Heinrich Kratzert. We knew each other from Memmingen. I also knew other mechanics from the same time. We greeted each other cordially, and I felt that the whole squadron was pleased that I had returned. On the first day, I was intensively instructed in the Ju 88. It was a far superior aircraft to the Do 17, which was the last aircraft I flew. Engine development had improved rapidly, with the result that the engines were more powerful. The two Jumo 211 engines had double the power of the Do 17 engines. This meant that the Ju 88 was more compact, and could carry a much greater bomb load. The observer's bomb sight instrument was much improved and completely new. The pilot also had a bomb sight, which he used when dive bombing. In a traversable glass turret were mounted twin machine-guns, which could be used all-round by the observer. Back to back with the pilot was the radio operator, who also had traversable twin machine-guns. Under the aircraft was another turret in which sat a gunner. The Ju 88 was conceived as a dual function aircraft for dive-bombing and for straight and level bombing. It was essential that the crew worked together, and to this end Teddy flew many practice flights with me and the radio operator, Flight

Sergeant Lubrich, and the gunner, Corporal Goerres, over the next few days. An advantage was that the crew were experienced, so I learned a lot in a short time. I was also given the opportunity to see Paris from the air, but the center was off limits, so we could only view the edge of the impressive city from a high altitude.

I was given new flying kit, warm, combined overalls, a life jacket with a small compass, and a bag with colored powder which glowed yellow. This was used when one landed in water so that it could be seen from the air. On the tenth day after my return, our crew was detailed for action against the enemy. The briefing was at 22:00 hrs on 16 October for the crews detailed for the action against London. We learned that a few minutes before we arrived, the target would be illuminated by a special bomb which left a light trail, so that the following bombers knew when to drop their bombs. These "light bombs" were dropped by specially designed, and fast, Ju 88s. At 23:32 hrs Teddy opened up the throttles and the engines roared. The brakes were released, and our Ju 88 began to roll. We had the identification number 9K+BD painted on the rear fusalage, but everything else was painted black, so that it was difficult to see the aircraft in the light of the searchlights. The aircraft increased speed on the runway, and Teddy ignited the booster rockets, which were necessary for take-off with a heavy bomb load. The undercarriage was up, and we were on our way. We carried two incendiary and two high explosive bombs, each weighing 500 kg. We climbed in a westerly direction to a height of 17,500 ft, which was our attack height, whereby at 13,000 ft we used our oxygen masks. From the start, I sat tensely in my seat with my map on my knees and stared into the darkness, trying to detect any enemy fighters. We neared the coast of England, which was sporadically lit up with probing searchlights between the clouds. Basically, there was radio silence during an attack. The radio operator listened out for the guide signals sent out from transmitters in France, and directed the way to our target. If the aircraft deviated to the right of the signal, a long pulsed signal was received. If the deviation was to the left, a rapid pulsed signal was heard.

Shortly after passing the coast of France, we came into the bad weather which had been forecast by the met. office. We flew above the clouds, and suddenly anti-aircraft shells burst near us. There were bright flashes of light, and briefly, small white clouds, then it was past. I learned the meaning of fear in these moments, though no one spoke about it during the entire duration of the attack. Lubrich reported to Teddy that he was about to receive the signal from the transmitters in Holland, or from a ship, that it was time to drop our bomb load. I had to activate the bombs with a switch. Lubrich confirmed this action, and as the signal was received, I released the bomb load, and our aircraft made a sort of "jump" as the bombs left. From the many explosions on the ground, we had an idea of the number of aircraft involved in this attack on London. The anti-aircraft fire intensified as we flew over the city center. Occassionly, the explosions of the flack could be heard when it was close by. Suddenly, Lubrich reported a night-fighter, left, and to our rear, so in spite of the bad weather night-fighters had taken off. Teddy made a steep diving left turn into the nearby welcome clouds and steered a course to the east. We could not fly too low, as there were barrage balloons, sometimes up to a height of 6,000 ft. During a later flight, we would make closer aquaintance with them. In the meantime, the bad weather front had moved eastwards, so that we were unable to make out the coast of France. Teddy ordered Lubrich to make radio contact with Etampes to ascertain the weather there and announce our estimated time of arrival. On 17 October at 02:16 hrs we landed and taxied to our dispersal point. Exhausted, I climbed out of the aircraft. I was congratulated by the three comrades for passing the test under fire. We then went to the debriefing room, and from there to the mess, where the rest of the crews who were involved in the attack on London were gathered. We celebrated my first action under fire until the early hours. The red wine ensured a good sleep until midday.

During lunch in the mess, we learned that the next attack on London was set for the coming night. I flew twelve night operations with Teddy to various targets, such as Birmingham and Glasgow, until 19 November, . On 15 November we were part of the large attacking force on Coventry. We started, between 01:00 and 02:00 hrs, as part of the 2nd wave. We carried high explosive bombs and two 1,000 kg air mines. About 30 miles from Coventry, we could see the red glow in the clouds, brighter than on my previous operations, where a large area of the city was on fire. For the first time, I shuddered at the thought of the people in the middle of this holocaust. My comrades seemed to be of the same opinion, since on the return journey there was no conversation other than that necessary when night fighters were spotted. After the debriefing, we gathered in the mess as usual, but in a very subdued mood due to this latest experience. Before I went to bed, I wrote my parents a letter describing the attack. I ended with the words "Should the enemy gain the upper hand and bomb our towns, then God help our people." At that time I could not imagine that the enemy, two years later, with larger four engined aircraft carrying a greater bomb load would do just that.

One night attack I flew with Wilhelm Rath, whose observer was ill. Teddy was given two days rest period. We flew at a height of 18,000 ft. Even so, we encountered heavy flack. We were lucky in that the flack exploded above our attacking height.

A few days before, as we were taking off, one of the take-off assisting rockets failed to ignite. The result was an abrupt break-away of the aircraft. In spite of the high take-off speed, Teddy reacted like lightning. He pressed the emergency rocket eject button, and the ejected rocket lay burning on the ground behind us. Full braking was being applied, but we shot futher into the darkness. We broke through a fence and came to a standstill a few yards from an anti-aircraft gun emplacement. We were all very white faced as we climbed out of the aircraft. However, shortly afterwards Teddy and I, together with two other comrades, sat in a Citroen car and drove towards Paris, where we would celebrate a birthday. One of the comrades was named Peter Brand, and the other man was Fritz Kuechle, known as "Old Fritz" due to his smart appearance and long service in an artillery regiment. Although he had only attended elementary school, he was recomended for the War College due to his outstanding ability. He transferred to the Luftwaffe, as did many others. Peter Brand knew his way around in Montmartre, and led us to a bar to which we descended via a spiral staircase to the cellar. Peter was greeted by the owner enthusiastically, as he was a constant guest there. He was previously the officer in charge of the group which selected the site for the airfield. As he had been stationed for a long time in or near Paris, he knew a few good restaurants. We were the only German soldiers in the bar, and in a good mood. The Frenchmen in the bar suggested that we take off our uniform jackets and ties. We hung our jackets over the bar stools, and celebrated brotherhood with the Frenchmen. Then we heard footsteps that could only belong to German "Authority." Four high ranking army civil servants entered the bar and took seats between Teddy and Peter. They were given their ordered drinks as Peter spoke our drinking saying "Cheers, where we belong, is in the air." We all drank to this, including the French patrons. Then, one of the civil servants with the rank of General Director spoke to Peter and asked "Gentlemen, are you German officers?" Peter answered, influenced by the wine, "Understand this, a couple of hours ago we were were in heavy flack over London, and it would be better, even for half civilized persons, if they did not disturb us." The gentlemen, feeling affronted, paid their bill and left. A short while later there appeared two military police sergeants. They asked to see our identity documents, the details of which they copied in their notebooks, and they informed us that a report would be submitted to the Paris Commander, because of our attitude to the civil servants. Peter reported to the commander the next morning, to inform him of the situation. A few days later, in the mess, Major Marienfeld told us, in a mischievous voice, that he had received a complaint from the Paris Commander, regarding our "misdemeanor." Our penalty was that we must pay the messbill for one evening. A penalty that we made without effort.

At the beginning of November our group was transferred to Bretigny. Lieutenant Bretschneider was promoted to Squadron-Leader and commanded number seven squdron, while I was given his position as adjudant to Marienfeld. I had a lot of work during the transfer and had to leave Teddy's crew. I now belonged to group headquarters and not to 8 squadron. Bretigny was some 25 miles from Etampes in a south-easterly direction, and nearer to Paris. The airfield commander was quartered in a barrack near the runway. His staff, which included me, were accommodated in a specially built barrack nearby, also near the runway.

In addition to my duties as adjudant, I also took over the position as transport officer, while it became known that I had held this position in Memmingen. The experienced Besendahl was also present in the transport group. He had heard that brand new Citroen cars were being given to units who applied for them. We drove there with an urgent order for five new cars issued by the commander. The cars were already camouflaged, and we had five drivers who drove the cars back to our airfield at Bretigny. Flight Sergeant Besendahl drove with me, and on the return journey we found a passable restaurant. As we sat at our table, we were joined by two men who, afer a while, asked us if the Citroen parked in front of the restaurant was ours. As I affirmed this, one of the men said that his business car had been confiscated by the French army at the beginning of hostilities. He was afraid to drive on the streets in his second car because it would be straight away requisitioned by the German army. The car was a Ford six cylinder cabriolet. He then asked us if it was possible to exchange his car for ours. After discussion with Besendahl as to how this could be accomplished, we drove with them to the garage where the Ford was. It was a dream car, and it looked like new. It was light beige with red leather upholstery. The owner gained the impression that we were to be trusted and confided to us that he was Jewish, which was another reason he could not be seen on the streets in the car. We arranged an exchange time at 01:00 hrs in the night. The Citroen had to be re-sprayed, then the Ford collected and straight away brought into the transport hangar to be re-sprayed in army camoflange colors. Besendahl told me the man was so grateful that he almost cried on my shoulder, and wished me a long life. It was a transaction that satisfied both parties.

While we so near Paris, we often visited the well known sights, such as the Arc de Triumph, Place de la Concorde, the Louvre, and the Opera House. We also had a look around in Montmartre. In Place Pigalle we found the world famous Variete Lido, and other "establishments" of interest. We, as young men, experienced many surprises. It was an unwritten law in our unit that we left together and returned together. This was naturally more secure, and no one was lost.

On a visit to Paris Peter Brand led us to an exclusive restaurant near the Exchange named "Au Canneton" (The Duck). Altogether we were six that sat at the table. The restaurant was not very large, and in the corner was a much decorated table, which one could not help seeing; obviously, an important guest was expected. We had just given our orders when in walked a number of civilians. To our great suprise, we saw, amongst them, our chief of staff, Reichsmarschall Hermann Göring, with two obvious bodyguards and two other men. Soon after Göring sat down, there appeared at our table one of the men. He introduced himself as the senior army doctor from Ondarza and said to Peter that the Reichsmarschall wished to know to which unit we belonged. Having obtained the information, he reported to Göring, who then invited us to join him at his table. He asked us many questions regarding our missions over England, and finally he said, "Gentlemen, you are my guests." With this we returned to our table. As we had ordered, we could only take advantage of his offer with dessert and drinks, which we did in no mean manner. We were impressed with his manner, but his very pale face surprised us. We later learned that he was a morphine addict, and Ondarza, also an addict, was constantly with him until the end of the war.

From the time I became adjutant, I flew with Teddy and his crew only until the end of November, as my new duties consumed a lot of time. Marienfeld dealt only with the more important matters, and left the rest for me to deal with. He was a devoted hunter, and in the lands belonging to the Escharcon castle there was ample opportunity for hunting. All group officers lived in the castle, which was also the mess. The castle belonged to the family Rothschild, and was generously furnished. In the large park were two lakes, in one of which lived wild ducks. There were also many pheasants throughout the park. Our doctor, Dr. Ott, was also a hunter, and often the two would go hunting. Thus, we often had duck, pheasant, hare, and deer on the menu, although Marienfeld never ate deer or venison.

Shortly before Christmas I was awarded the Iron-Cross 1st class for my operations over England. In addition, I was given a week's leave. I let Kaethe know, and she traveled to Geislingen, since naturally, I wanted to see as much of the family as possible.

My suitcases were packed with good things like V.S.O.P. Cognac, Champagne, Goose-liver pate, Cointreau, and Grand Marnier, together with dessous for the ladies. I traveled on the fast night train from the Gare d Ouest, via Stuttgart, and eventually home. It was to be a long time before I made a journey home again.

At the beginning of January I had to be in Bretigny, while Marienfeld would be away for a few days. I had obtained permission to re-train on the Ju 88, since for the forthcoming operations I wanted to be an aircraft captain, with my own crew. At first, I flew the He 111, which was used by the group as transport aircraft. Then I completed a three week course in Landsberg for blind flying, so that I could request the blind flying permission. After returning from the course, I continued with my training on the Ju 88.

As adjutant, I also commanded the reconnaissance group. This consisted of "other ranks," plus a chief technician who, with his mechanics, was responsible for the servicing of the transport and aircraft used by the Commander, Adjutant, and Technical Officers. Four Ju 88s, one He 111, and an Me 108, together with the transport unit, completed the reconnaissance group.

Marienfeld ensured that I had the opportunity to fly many courier and travel flights. I was also given a lot of experience in bad weather flying. With the He 111 I could often fly to Memmingen and Oberwiesenfeld. In the meantime, I concerned myself with selecting a crew. Wilhelm Rath had disiplinary problems with his radio operator, Kurt Boettcher. As he had taken another operator for his crew, he suggested that I make use of an experienced operator like Boettcher, who was usually refered to as "Bubi." He was willing to fly with me, and asked if I would accept private Gallermann as gunner in my crew. Rath also wanted to change his driver, so I took him as my driver. In this way Flight Sergeant Haupt was transferred to the Reconnaissance Unit and was my driver until the end of my time with the squadron. Since we were a newly found crew, we flew many familiarizing training flights. We now needed an observer to complete the crew. I had a man who, after high-school exams, wanted to study physics, but was enlisted into the army. I asked him if, after short period of training by an experienced observer, he would join my crew. He was impressed and answered in the affirmative. Heinz Ernst, due to his ability in mathematics, soon became an excellent observer. He showed the traditional traits of a Frieslander, in that he was often slow, but thorough, and he never seemed to "flip-out." He was always at ease and never shocked at anything. A Squadron-Leader arrived from the Air War School to learn about night operations against England. He flew a few times with us, then I had to fly him to Greifswald, where he was taking over a new unit. I obtained permission from Marienfeld to stop off at Werder on the return journey. On 24 March I flew to Greifswald and Neumuenster to drop off a comrade with my now complete crew. After landing, I was cordially greeted by the instructors I knew. On 26 March I came from the "Met" office and headed for my He 111. On the way I met a previous cadet, Marseille, who was now a captain and squadron commander in the Africa-Corps. We were extremly pleased to see each other again, though there was little time for conversation. Good wishes were said as we were both going on our separate ways, I to France and he to Tunis. Marseille was killed a short while later. On the return journey from Werder to Bretigny we encountered a bad weather front, which meant that we had to fly in the clouds. For the first time we flew without a co-pilot for over three hours in the "pea-soup," as thick clouds were called. It was an advantage that Bubi had a lot of experience, because through exact compass use he brought us directly over Bretigny, as we saw as we decended through the clouds. We taxied to the dispersal area, and Bubi said "Captain, the crew have complete trust in you. That was a perfect blind flying trip, and that with little experience."

On our return, I learned that the complete group was to be transferred to Weiner-Neustadt, and were therefore deep in the preparations. My order was to fly there in three days time, with a stop-over in Memmingen. We started on 29 March and flew to Memmingen, where we would pick up a passenger, the 1a, a Lieutenant Fritsch. He was on holiday in Metzingen, but would return the next day. I had, therefore, the opportunity to spend a night with my family, shortly before the birth of our daughter, Ingrid.

13

TRANSFER EASTWARDS

On 30 March we flew from Memmingen to the large airfield at Wiener-Neustadt with our 1A, Alfred Fritsch. The flight took two hours. There was also a factory on the edge of the airfield which produced the Me 109 fighter. This was the predominant fighter aircraft for all fighter squadrons. With us arrived a advance detachment unit of a fighter-bomber squdron with Me 110 aircraft. Our III./51 was opposite the command-post. There we would be accommodated in several barracks. Alfred and I could now concentrate, with help from futher arrivals from Bretigny, on the arrival of the ground personnel, who would be coming by train.

After only a few days—the 11th and 12th, to be exact—as a new crew, we could take delivery of a factory new aircraft; the Ju 88 9K-FD., in which we practiced one engine flying, together with diving. Shortly before, in another Ju 88, I had a slight mishap, my one and only. As I was on approach to land, I reduced speed too soon, and the aircraft dropped a few feet. Both tires burst and flew off, and the undercarriage also suffered. The damage could be repaired by the ground crew in the hangar. Even so, it hurt to realize that I had made such a simple mistake.

While Poland and France were quickly occupied, Denmark and Norway were almost in German hands, and Rommel, with the Italians, had successes in North Africa. On April 12th, however, we were suddenly placed on alert. We were told that an invasion of Yugoslavia and Greece, along with its islands, was planned. My crew and I were ready. My aircraft was the first in the wave, which was controlled by Fritz Kuechle. The attack was to be in horizontal flight over the target, which was a military barracks near Mostar. Heinz had his first opportunity to use the new bomb sight and drop the bombs. We flew in good visibility at a height of 13,000 ft.

The target was easily seen, and was eliminated by the attacking aircraft. There were no fighter aircraft to contend with, but the strong flack caused us some problems. During the daytime the flack explosions could be seen, and because there was so much, one had the impression of flying through clouds. We landed undamaged after three and a half hours in Wiener-Neustadt. The crew had had their first experience under operational conditions.

On my 25th birthday there were two futher air attacks on military positions near Mostar. This time we were on the right wing of Marienfeld. In the second attack, for the first time, I would use the dive bomb sight and drop the bombs. The target was a military convoy with tanks. After the bombs were dropped we climbed high, and we could see that our bombs had hit the target. Our gunner had the opportunity to use the camera to record our target accuracy. It was a specially designed camera for filming from the air with the name Robot, which was very similar to a Leica. The pictures were amazingly sharp, and with the aid of such photographs, the results of an attack could be determined. The attack on Yugoslavia was quickly over, mainly due to the huge air attacks. Despite the heavy flak and machine-gun fire, few aircraft were damaged. Thank God that no one from our group was injured.

New orders arrived, but we could not, at the time, see the sense of them. All aircraft were to be fitted with new bomb carriers, in the bomb-bay. We called them "rubbish containers," because therein 750 fragmentation bombs could be carried, each weighing two kilograms. These were to be dropped when flying at a low level. The detonator was activated after the bomb had left the aircraft by a small propeller that rotated due to the wind. When the correct speed was achieved, the bomb was "live" and the propeller dropped off. This meant lots of training in low level flying. In order to cause as little disturbance as possible to the local residents, we practiced over the Pussta in Hungary. During a practice flight we lost our comrade Maletz and his crew. Although he was an experienced pilot, he made a mis-judgment in flight, hit a poplar tree with the wings, and crashed into a field. The crew's graves are in the cemetary of Wiener-Neustadt.

In our free time we visited the sights in the beautiful city of Vienna. The cathedral made a deep impression on me.

Two pubs were often visited by us, the "Candle Parlour" and the "Heurigen-Wirtschaften." A special attraction was our outing to the Semmering. On the advice of Lieutenant Capesius (known as Caps), who came from Graz, we entered the first building in the square, the Palace-Hotel. We were seven men altogether, and we drove there in two cars. We entered the dining room and found places at a table. It soon became obvious that in spite of the shortage of food, we could see from the menu that there was a large choice of meals that could actually be served. An excellent meal was had by all, and we all agreed that it could not be better in France. Afterwards, we sat at the bar and could not help noticing that there were quite a number of good looking and well dressed young ladies staying at the hotel. It turned out that many were the wives of highly placed persons who, due to the bombing of their home towns, were safer in the hotel. Several comrades flirted with the ladies and drank quite a lot. Our two drivers, of course, did not drink. I was one of them.

As soon as the opportunity arrived, we drove to the Semering again. I was accompanied by Peter Brand, Wilhelm Rath, and Fritz Kuechle. We saw on arrival that the hotel car park was almost full with police cars, and at the entrance to the hotel were two armed guards. As we entered the hotel, the guards presented arms. We could not understand what was going on, but in the hotel foyer the manager approached us and explained that the Reichsmarschall Göring, together with his staff, was staying in the hotel. He then wanted to know whether we would be staying. We thought that as Göring knew us he would have no objection to our being in the same hotel. The time for the evening dinner arrived, and we made our way to the dining room. At a large table near the window, with a magnificent view of the mountains, sat Göring and his staff. We bowed slightly in his direction and sat down at a table that was reserved for us. No sooner had we done so, than Ondarz came to our table and asked us if we would honor the Reichsmarschall by joining him at his table. This time we had to describe our attacks on Yugoslavia. He seemed to be satisfied with our descriptions, and said that we were his guests. We thanked him and returned to our table. This time we ordered the best that the hotel had to offer, and after a sumptuous meal, we made our way to the bar. As we sat at the bar, the barkeeper came to us and whispered, "A message from the chief, all drinks are free, as long as you pay attention to the lonely ladies who live in the hotel." Years later, we learned the reason for the generous gesture. In 1943 the manager and his daughter were arrested by the security police on the suspicion that they had helped the enemy to infiltrate young women into the hotel who then mixed with the other ladies. The aim was to listen to conversations for any military information which could be passed on. Whether anyone from our group was in any way involved we never knew, especially as many who were there were later killed, or missing in action.

Practice and courier flights were predominant in May. Until the beginning of June nothing unusual happened, except that we took delivery of many new Ju 88 aircraft.

On 17 June we received the order to move to an airfield named Lezany, in East Poland. It was near the river Bug, which was the border between Poland and Russia. During the night, all technicians and armaments personnel were flown to Poland in transport aircraft. The start for the whole group was planned for 18 August

14

HITLER ORDERS THE ATTACK ON RUSSIA

I was given the order from Marienfield to fly the first contingent to Lezany and commence with the organization. During the night the group's 1a received new maps of the border and inland of Russia. From the maps we could see that a number of Russian airfields were either complete or under construction. My crew knew nothing of the approaching tasks. "Why are you so thoughtful today," asked Heinz. "Secret command matters," I answered. "You will find out soon enough." They had, of course, an idea of what the future held. Bubi, although strict radio silence was observed, tuned into Radio Belgrade, which transmitted dance music and the news. During the flight over Poland's rather flat land it became obvious to me why we would carry the fragmentation bombs and had practiced low-level flying. It was in preparation for attacks on airfields and troop movements.

The 1st group were moved to a Rumainian airfield for operations in the Mediterranean area, and it became clear where we would be operating.

The Lezany airfield was to the East of the town, in a large flat area of land, hardly camouflaged and with few shelters for the aircraft. This I took in hand, in that I would have the shelters completed and more built. To this end I approached the local mayor for workers. Strange as it may now seem, he directed me to the Jewish council, who, to our great surprise, said that when they were needed they were available. The workers would be paid by us, but that did not worry us. In three days the shelters for the Ju 88s were completed. Some were even roofed over to enable repairs to be carried out. As we, years later, learned how the SD, Gestapo, and police had treated these families, we were agast, sad, and angry. We could not undertake any action against them, because we were hundreds of miles to the East and did not know anything at that time about what was going on in the West.

Together with Marienfeld, who was now a Lieutenant Colonel, and Alfred Fritsch, I flew on the 21st in an Me 108 to the division's operations room. General Pflugbeil, the division commander, informed all the group's leaders and their staff of the plans for the coming attack on Russia. Every group leader was given detailed orders regarding the target.

What we could expect in regard to Russian air defenses was not known. What was known was that many new airfields had been, and were being, constructed. Our reconnaisance aircraft had reported numerous troop movements along the border and futher inland.

Our group was given the order to attack the enemy airfields and destroy the bomber and fighter aircraft thereon. This was to be a low level attack.

With a surprise attack in the early morning, it was hoped that a minimum of defense action could be expected. On the return flight to Lezany from the meeting, we discussed the orders that Marienfeld had to give the squadron commanders and the technical units.

In a provisional mess, converted out of an old building on the airfield, we sat together and discussed the problems that the next day would bring. The atmosphere was not conducive to laughter.

After a rest pause—since sleep was out of the question—the targets were detailed by the commanders. During the night a conference was held to discuss the attack on what was for us a completely unknown enemy. Marienfield took the opportunity to announce Hitler's order to all commanders of the army, navy, and air force, which was that from 22 June 1941 Russia would be attacked. This was to prevent the spread of communism.

Full of confidence and convinced that a necessary war was being fought, the crews made their way to their aircraft. Each squadron would attack a different airfield, at which our reconnisance aircraft had determined that a large number of aircraft were on the ground. The airfields had been photographed so that we could see where the aircraft were on the ground. Alfred Fritsch, the 1a, and myself were ordered to ensure that on the return of our aircraft, they were re-fueled, re-armed, and the bomb bay loaded.

Dawn was breaking as the first wing of the 7th squadron took off with earsplitting engine noise. They climbed steeply and headed East. Altogether there were 26 Ju 88 aircraft, each loaded with 720 fragmentation bombs.

We, and the rest of us who were not flying, had our orders that came into action on the return of the aircraft.

As usual, during an attack, radio silence was observed. It would be between one and one and a half hours before the first wave landed. We waited, in a strained manner, in the operations room for the first contact with our aircraft. We knew that a high risk was attached to low flying operations with the new two kilogram bombs. What the enemy had for air defenses, as well as the quality and the number thereof, we had no knowlege.

After a good hour, the first report came from a crew, about to land, whose aircraft had received many hits. We drove to the dispersal in order to question the crew, and there were many hits from small arms fire in the under-wings and the tail. From this we deduced that the ground defense was strong. In the following hours only 20 aircraft returned, one of the last being Marienfeld. He entered the operations room with his crew, looking tired, and gave his version of the first attack. In the meantime, Alfred Fritsch and I had the reports from already landed crews. They reported huge damage to aircraft on the ground, both fighters and bombers. Circulating over the enemy airfields were a number of fighters of the "Rata" type, and on the bombing run our aircraft were fired upon by twin machine guns and flack. Some aircraft had to return on one engine, but landed successfully. Three hours after the attack, it was clear that six aircraft had been lost. From the reports of the experienced pilots and observers, it was determined that much damage had been done to the enemy aircraft on the ground. Many were completely destroyed, and many more were severly damaged. Few enemy aircraft were able to take off, thus the surprise attack was a success. The crews were also attacked by the "Ratas" in flight, but they were beaten off by the firepower of our gunners.

We learned, per teleprinter, that around midday we would be given information regarding the next operation. We feverishly worked on the aircraft to prepare as many as possible for the next attack.

For the second attack, Marienfeld put me and my crew on his right wing. We would be attacking troop accommodation tents, vehicles, and troop columns. Just after 14:00 hrs we took off, flew in a Westerly direction, and climbed to six and a half thousand feet, to take advantage of the cloud cover. Then we turned East and headed for our target. We flew in a tightly packed formation for better defense against enemy aircraft. During low-level attacks one had to fly independently, so to this end we flew behind Marienfeld for the attack.

Each aircraft, having left the cloud cover, had to find an appropriate target during a steep glide to the operational level. The observer Heinz and radio operator Bubi had good eyesight, and reported that directly in front of us was a tented area with a lot of Russian army personel nearby. With a left diving turn, I headed for the target. Over the first tents I dropped the bombs, which exploded in line, directly on the target. Gallermann cried "Everything is destroyed." We were machine-gunned by the air defenses, which until then we had not noticed. We were subjected to this fire the whole time of our attack. Gallermann fired continuously with his twin machine-guns in the belly of the aircraft. I climbed and saw Marienfeld's aircraft, also in a steep climb. I opened the throttles and repositioned my aircraft on his right wing again. Shortly before the river Bug we spotted a military convoy of lorries and tankers. Over the radio, Marienfeld ordered the attack on the convoy. With only machine-guns we attacked. Marienfeld flew in the lead at about 60 ft with all guns firing. Soon explosions were seen. Then we flew over the column, also with all guns firing. I climbed steeply to aviod the enemy fire, and Marienfeld gave the order to return to base. He had decided to fly another attack alone on the convoy. As we were on the return journey, it was only possible for Bubi to follow Marienfeld's attack. Suddenly, he cried "The right-hand engine is on fire." An hour after we had taken off we landed. We had received many shots from machine-guns and rifle fire, but luckily nothing important had been hit. In two hours our aircraft was again operational. We, naturally, kept an eye open for the return of Marienfeld's aircraft. That he had not yet returned, we assumed was due to the damage to the right engine which Bubi had seen on fire. We started on our second attack around 18:00 hrs. The order was to attack airfields in the area of Tarnopol. Again, at low level, bombs were dropped and a nearby tented area was destroyed. The flack was all around us, and made one feel uncomfortable. There was only one thought in mind, get out of here quickly. Seconds seemed like eternity. During later attacks one had learned to come to terms with the defenses. We were also attacked with machine-gun fire from the ground and many "Ratas" in the air, which flew around like wasps. These aircraft had been used by the communists in the Spanish civil war. Again we attacked independently. Each aircraft was on its own. We received many hits from the ground, including a flack hit on our rudder. On landing we learned that the damage was not repairable, so the aircraft would be used for spares.

The results of the first few days was not good for our group. Six crews did not return. Depressed, we sat in the mess until Fritz Kuechle produced a couple of bottles of wine that were left over from the move from France. With the consumption thereof we felt in a better mood. Our "Old Fritz" would never be forgotten for the way he danced the Krakoviac on the table at midnight, and sang "Comrades, where we belong is in the air." In the early hours of 23 July he flew on a mission. He never returned.

Two days later we took delivery of a new Ju 88 "9K-ED." With it we started on 25 July at 05:00 hrs as wingman of Sergeant Mueller. The target was the same as before, destroy aircraft on the ground at Tarnopol airfield. Mueller was a most experienced pilot, with most of his experience gained during attacks over France and England. At 6,500 ft there was some slight cloud cover, and we flew in an Easterly direction. The view of the ground was enough to see the target. We dropped through the clouds, and Heint and Bubi began to count. In front there were 8, 10, 15—no, many more, upwards of 20 fighters. Again these Ratas circled above and in front of us. It seemed that we had been detected by their "early warning" system. Without hesitation I dived vertically towards the ground. In the rear-view mirror I saw that Mueller was climbing in an attempt to reach the cloud cover, followed by the Ratas. We were a few hundred feet from the ground as Bubi shouted that Mueller's aircraft was on fire and in a steep dive, and it hit the ground. Why Mueller had attempted to climb, instead of diving, I will never know. There was not time to think about it, as I saw in front of us a row of Martin bombers in front of a hangar. I came down to 60 ft and let go the bombs. Michael cried that there were direct hits, and the Martins were destroyed. The ground personnel, who were refueling, sprang for cover. Bubi suddenly reported fighters behind us. In the rear view mirror I saw several Ratas which appeared to be out to get us. To turn and fly in a Westerly direction was out of the question, as they blocked the way. In an attempt at evasion, I flew nearer the ground, and as fast as possible. Bubi fired his guns when a Rata came too near. They attacked us from above and from behind. There were flashes of fire as they fired from above, but most of the shells landed on the ground. Ratas that were behind us and not visible to me were seen by Bubi, who directed me left or right to avoid their fire. The machine-gun fire from the fighters behind suddenly increased. It was only too clear to see in my rear-view mirror. This could be dangerous; Bubi's guns had become blocked, and he started to look for the reason. Luckily, this was soon cleared. Michel was first to realize what was wrong, and shouted to Bubi to open the bullet pod, which collected the used bullet cases. Bubi reacted it quickly, and they fell to the floor. Thereafter his guns functioned again. Two Ratas were hit by bullets from Bubi's guns and caught fire. During such moments one had no feeling of time, only the faint hope of eluding the fighters using all the tricks available. I made a small course correction to avoid flying too far East, which would mean we would not have enough fuel for the return journey. Before us was a small hill, and as we flew over the ridge I flew steeply lower and suddenly made a left curve and climbed steeply in an effort to reach the cloud cover.

The fighter pilots were so suprised at the move that they flew straight on. We climbed with wide open throttles. Bubi had the fighters in view. They had turned and were also climbing to attack us. He gave the closing distance, 500, 400, 300, 200, 100 meters. At 100 meters we suddenly disappeared from their view into the protective clouds. Unable to see, the fighters were no longer a threat to us. Covered in sweat, but no longer filled with fear, we skipped from cumulous to cumulous cloud. We had lost the attackers. After two hours I prepared to land; the wheels came down, but the wing flaps could not be operated. The hydraulic system was probably shot to pieces. We made the approach too fast, and directly on the edge of the runway we touched down. I then discovered that the brakes did not function. We rolled over the opposite end of the runway and ended up in a field. This was our second "runaway." We were all happy that we were still in one piece, and started to count the number of hits we had collected. One in particular had hit a fuel tank, but due to the special covering had not penetrated it. One wheel had also a flat tire.

We were shocked to learn that we seemed to be the only crew to return from the operation. Rather depressed, we went to our quarters. Then we received the good news that Marienfeld, with his crew, were all right. He had reported from the operations room of an army division. His engines had both been hit, and he crash landed on a sandbank in the river Bug and was rescued by army infantrymen. As I had not anticipated the return of our commander, I had, as adjutant, already packed his suitcases, although his return was to be short lived.

Our 1a, Alfred Fritsch, was a reserve officer who was not afraid of his superiors. He reported to the group's headquarters the successes and the losses, with the suggestion that low-level attacks be discontinued, as the expected losses would be too great. Not just our group, but groups 1 and 2 also had heavy losses. In spite of this, low-level attacks were again ordered for the next day, and again there were heavy losses The General of the air force, von Greim, then decided to cancel low-level attacks. Up to this point, the squadrons had lost nearly half of their aircraft and crews.

Futher operations were flown at high level. We carried a bomb load of 50, 250, or 500 kg bombs, depending on the target to be attacked. From 1 July we flew three operations of this type.

On 26 July I received the order to fly to Memmingen, with the instruction to visit and console the wives of our fallen, or missing, comrades. Such a task hit me hard. I flew in a He 111 with Heinrich Kratzert, our chief repair man, and Bubi. We were also accompanied by an officer from group headquarters. Unfortunately, I missed Kaethe, as she and our small daughter, Ingrid, were visiting her mother.

To the wives, whom I knew well, I had to break the sad news. It was the most difficult thing I had encountered in my career as a soldier. Most of all the fate of Fritz Kaechle's mother, since her husband had not returned from the first world war, and now her son would not return from this war. But there was little time for thinking things over, as on the following day we had to return to Lezany.

During the next few days a few of the crews of missing aircraft turned up. Most of their aircraft had received effective ground defense hits to the engines and had to crash-land. The advance of our army was so rapid that the crews did not have to spend much time concealed in the woods before our troops found them. Ten days later, the town of Tarnopol was captured. In the prison, a barbaric act of revenge was found, which we would not have thought possible. Some of our comrades had been tortured in a most bestial manner. They had been blinded, and their ears and genitals had been brutally cut off. Most had broken arms and legs, too. It was left to our unit's doctor to identify them from the dental photos. Our photographer documented everything. Although we were witnesses to this, there are still people who do not believe, or will not accept it, as fact. As the news of the tortured men became widespread, the consequences for the future had an effect on our comrades. A Major Serschen had to make a crash landing after an attack. He was trapped in the pilot's seat and could not run and hide. The observer and the radio operator were able to run and conceal themselves in a cornfield, where they saw how the Asiatic enemy troops stormed the Ju and brutally massacred their pilot, the worst being his screams of pain. The two men in the cornfield did not have to wait long before rescue was at hand, since the advancing army reconnaisance troops found them. They were still trembling from the horror they had witnessed. They had to undergo therapy during a long convalescence. Many comrades carried a poison with them, to aviod being in enemy captivity. I and my crew decided that if worst came to worst by a crash landing and we were detected, we would defend ourselves until the last, but one bullet was left to use on ourselves. When there were no longer Asiatic troops to contend with, parachuted aircrews, as well as crash landed crews were captured by the Russians and interned, without being tortured and killed.

We returned after the fifth attack after hostilities commenced on a road traffic congestion point, only to learn that we were once again to be transferred. This time to the airfield Vlodimiercz.

The operations room was to be found in a large tent. Personnel were also accommodated in large tents. I had, in a department store in Paris, bought a small tent for which I now had a use. It was sprayed with camoflage paint, which also made it waterproof. It also had a porch that gave shelter from the sun. I now had my own "house." We furnished, from bomb and engine boxes, a tent which would be our mess. Meals were produced out of what could be found, until Alfred Schwager and private Reinbold took over. The latter owned a gentlemen's clothing shop in his civilian life. They handled the cooking, although in the beginning we only noticed an improvement in the fruit availability.

Vlodimiercz lay southeast from Tarnopol. The climate was sub-tropical, so that we were mainly dressed in appropriate clothing. When we flew, we wore the normal flying clothing. Altogether we flew 12 operations, mostly against road troop movements, in order to destroy the enemy's supply requirements and hinder the retreating troops. Sometimes we supported our tanks in their advance. There was little enemy air activity against us, but we encountered a lot of flack, which gave us quite a shock at times.

Due to the heavy losses during the low-level attacks, we flew to our old airfield at Wiener-Neustadt, where we received fresh crews and new aircraft, the Ju 88 A3. This time I flew with the commander in his Ju while the rest of my crew flew in the He 111. During the time at Wiener-Neustadt, much material and spares had to be collected from Memmingen. This provided an opportunity to see Kaethe and our small daughter, Ingrid. They had worried about me, since so many comrades had failed to return from an operation. We did not have much time together because I, as adjutant, had a lot of work was waiting for me, especially as the commander was away for a few days on leave.

From Wiener-Neustadt we visited the hotel in the Semmering, as well as the city of Vienna.

Lieutenant Bender spent most of the time in the gaming rooms of the Casino in Baden, near Vienna. He seemed to have a lucky streak, as he won quite a lot of money. I accompanied him once and promptly lost my stake money. That was enough for me; avoiding the temptation to play futher, I left and returned to camp. Bender did not have the opportunity to spend his gains on his next leave as he intended, because he was killed in action just after we returned to the East at the end of August.

15

RETURN TO THE FRONT IN THE ADVANCE ON RUSSIA

Once again we left our homeland on 28 April, fresh from our four week's pause. We landed at the airfield at Balti-Ost, and found there were new crews and new aircraft in addition to the overhauled and repaired ones. The 2 kg bomb retainers were removed, and the usual ones were refitted. From now on it would be altitude bombing, or dive bombing. We did not know what awaited us this time, after the disasterous first attacks at the end of June to the beginning of July. Of the many shot down in these attacks, very few returned. Some remained hidden until German troops appeared. Altogether there were 30 missing, and very few returned.

This time we flew the 300 km eastward for two and a half hours to the airfield at Balti-Ost. The airfield was in a cultivated plain in Bessarabia. It actually belonged to Rumania, but had been annexed by Russia, like so many other border areas. There were a few buildings standing, which we converted for use for the airfield controller, flight control, and operations room. As there were other buildings available, we made one the mess and used the others as our accommodations. Other personnel were accommodated in large tents. We were not far from the Black Sea, so the climate was almost sub-tropical. During the day it was very hot, and at night it became quite cool. The humidity was also very high, due to the nearness of the sea.

In the following weeks we flew 30 operations in large groups. Each operation had no less than nine, but mostly between 12 and 18 aircraft. In formation we could defend ourselves against the new Russian fighters, the MiGs. They were more maneuverable, faster, and better armed than the Ratas. The name came from the constructors Mikojan and Gurewitsch. Our orders were to attack trains, road junctions, and troop convoys in support of the advance of our troops. There were also attacks on harbor installations in the Black sea, which were well defended with anti-aircraft guns. We sustained hits, even at a high altitude. The explosive material seemed to be of poor quality, which was lucky for us, as we received two hits on the rear and more hits on the wings and tail asembly. During the repairs, it was found that the shell fragments did not have much penetration power. During these operations we lost few crews.

Lieutenant Rudi Bretschneider was very unfortunate, in that he had to crash land after a low-level attack on 22 June. For 14 days he hid in cornfields and woods until he stumbled on German troops and was returned to our group. During the next attack, he received hits on an engine, which caused him to crash-land again. Again, he landed in enemy territory. His return coincided with a visit to our group by General Ritter von Greim. Rudi reported that his right engine had been hit by flack at low level and put out of action. He crash-landed in a field nearby. Minutes later he and his crew saw a Russian army patrol advancing towards them wildly firing their machine guns. At this moment the radio operator let loose the dinghy that was stowed in the rear of the aircraft and used for rescue after crash-landings in the sea. The dinghy is inflated by compressed air, which is automatically done when it is released from the aircraft. The sudden appearance of a yellow "monster" from the rear of the aircraft effected such a shock on the enemy that they ran away in fear. The crew then removed the three twin machine guns from the aircraft and positioned them defensively. "We had agreed that we would defend ourselves until the last bullet so that we would not end up as prisoners. Luckily, a Rumanian tank vehicle found us, and we were safe."

Bretschneider looked years older after these two experiences, so much so that the general immediately granted him four weeks leave. He also forbade futher air operations. He would arrange that a different employment be found for the whole crew. In this way Bretschneider survived the war. He attended the Academy and ended up as a general staff officer.

A heavy attack was planned for 24 September on the headquarters of the Russian fighting forces. These headquarters were situated in Perekop, which was on land that joined the island of Krim with the mainland. This time our 1a, Albert Fritsch, flew with us as observer. We were in the last wave of aircraft, and I had to fly through middle to heavy flack. I flew in a steep glide to the target, which we could see through the smoke from explosions on the ground. At low level we dropped our 250 and 500 kg bombs. I then climbed steeply. With the robot camera, Michel photographed the heavily damaged headquarters. A short time later there appeared in the magazine "Illustrierter Beobachter" (Photo Observations) our photograph.

The magazine was printed by the NSDAP. How they obtained the photo, we never found out. We felt, not surprisingly, very bittter about this.

An interesting situation arose in that the local Gypsies wanted to barter their fruit, chickens, and anything else eatable, in exchange for cigarettes and spirits. Once we received a visit from a Gypsy family. The oldest member offered to tell our fortunes in exchange for cigarettes. As well as other comrades, captain Zeep was prophesied that he would have a long life and many children. As the younger girls started to dance for the soldiers, the grandmother said that they should dance topless. This the soldiers appreciated so much that they gave them cigarettes, spirits, and bread. Pictures of the dancing beauties were publicized in many articles.

As I write this part of my book, there is, on television, a program showing these pictures—quite a coincidence. The commentary, however, I think is totally incorrect. It said that all these people were killed during the war. So long as the gypsies lived in their camp near the airfield, I and my comrades can swear that not one was ever mishandled by us. This just shows how the media, without proper research, but because it deals with the wartime generation, are ready to insult them. Bismark had a saying about this, "Journalisim is the trade of a failed existence."

How differently were the actions of the Russian soldiers in east Germany, in east and west Preussen, in Pommern, in Schlesien, and in middle Germany. To say nothing of Poland and Czechoslovakia.

Not only did we have to contend with the high humidity, but also with a plague of field mice. They were everywhere, in our tents, even in our shoes. A newcomer to our group was Lieutenant Kielhorn, who shared my tent. He had a small caliber pistol, and one evening he shot 11 mice who were climbing up the curtains.

The front advanced so rapidly eastwards that the distance increased for our supporting flights. With this in mind, we were transferred to an airfield named Nikolajev. Here there were no signs of air attacks. All the buildings and runway were intact. We occupied the airfield on 27 October, and at last, after a long time, were able to live in better accommodations. This was important in view of the forthcoming winter. Even so, we found that we had exchanged the fieldmice for lice, which were no better, if not worse. I was again bunkered with Kielhorn. During the nights he was bitten all over by our unwanted guests, while I received not one bite. He must have had "sweet blood," as the saying goes. I put my unbitten nights down to the fact that these bugs did not like alcohol as much as I did. In other respects, the accomodations were not too bad.

Many of our attacks were directed against targets on the island of Krim. Many dive bombing attacks were made on the harbor installations of Kertsch, also in Krim. It covered a very large area which lay between Asowschem and the Black sea. Kertsch and Sevastopol, situated on the west side, were heavily defended by anti-aircraft guns. During our first dive bombing attacks on 10 November we encountered so much flack that it was decided future attacks would be made in shallow dives. This enabled speeds of up to 600 km to be reached, which made defensive fire more difficult. The pilot naturally controlled the dive and used the air-brakes to slow the aircraft down when the target was reached. This allowed the bomb-aimer more time to select his target. A big disadvantage was that the enemy attackers had a better chance of success. With a more shallow dive and at high speed, the disadvantage was minimized, so it was decided by experienced pilots that in order to keep losses down to a minimum, it was better to gauge the situation first before committing the aircraft and crew.

We were given the order on 16 November that our crew should attack a destroyer which was at anchor in Sevastopol harbor. The cloud cover was in our favor as we approached the target. We flew at 16,000 ft, and through a gap in the clouds our observer Heinz saw two destroyers anchored next to each other. The destroyers were in a fjord. On both sides were cliffs and hills to a height of some 2,000 ft. It was an ideal natural defense. From a southeasterly direction I put the aircraft into a steep dive with the engines at full power.

When I had both ships in the bombsight at a height of 2,000 ft, I let go the 1,000 kg special penetrating bomb for attacking ships, and a 500 kg bomb. We continued to fly lower, and Michel reported a direct hit, which he photographed. I then climbed steeply, and we were suddenly surrounded by flack from every gun caliber imaginable. It was a regular fireworks display we flew through. The guns were positioned on the hillsides around the harbor. I flew lower in a westerly direction so that we were now lower than the anti-aircraft guns, and in this way we avoided more flack, since the guns could not shoot downwards. After we landed we found we had been hit in the tailplane, which, luckily, had not affected the steering capability. During a lone attack on anti-aircraft gun installations near Schachty, which was the center of a coal mining district, we received 20 hits. The repaired Ju was available, the Ju 88-9K+ED. With this aircraft we flew, again alone, an attack on troop concentrations in the Schachty area. We flew just above the clouds' lower layers, at 3,000 ft in the direction of the front line. Now and again we flew lower than the clouds to observe the ground and find a target. To our left we saw a large assembly of lorries and enemy soldiers. Immediately we climbed into the clouds and flew almost blind. We used a stopwatch to gauge the distance. Three minutes straight flying, then a 180 degree turn, then a futher three minutes in straight flight. Cautiously we left the cloud cover, and there in front of us was our target. The lorries and men were between farm buildings and mixed with farm carts and other farm implements. I dropped our bomb load of ten 50 kg bombs and four 250 kg bombs directly over the farm complex. In the rear view mirror I could see that we had scored direct hits. We were at a height of 60ft. Michel said something, but I did not hear anything any more. When I came to, I saw through blurred eyes that our aircraft was in a shallow glide. I managed to pull it up to 2,000 ft and through the clouds, mainly due to our high attack speed. I learned later that I had been hit. I could not move my left knee, and my left hand was like a fist which I could not open. A shell had penetrated the aircraft cabin and exploded. Heinz had taken over the emergency controls for height and turning. He found a hole in my combination-suit next to my left knee, from which blood flowed, and also my left arm was also bleeding. He bandaged the wounds, strapped my arm to my chest, and bound my right foot on the rudder pedal, since I could move the right leg. In this manner I could steer the aircraft. Bubi had made contact with the nearest airfield on our side of the frontline, which was Taganrog. He asked for landing permission, as the pilot was wounded. We carried with us a few important medical items, and after I had taken a pain killer tablet, chewed a coffee bean, and drunk a large cognac, I felt a bit better and decided to fly to our home base at Nikolajev airfield instead. I was able to climb slowly, since at a greater height we had a better chance of finding somewhere on the ground to make a forced landing, should it be necessary. Everything went well, and after three and three-quarters of an hour, we prepared to land. As I could not operate the throttles or the levers for lowering the wheels and flaps, I gave Bubi the necessary instructions when required. I flew low, and at the touchdown point on the runway, I gave Bubi the order to reduce the engine speed with the throttles. It was a successful landing, and we taxied to our dispersal and shut down. Now that the stress was removed, I felt pain. Heinz and Bubi lifted me out of the aircraft, Lieutenant Wolf, the technical officer, was ready with his transport to take me to the air force field hospital, which luckily was also stationed at Nikolajew. The pain had now increased, especially in my right eye. Those who know the state of the roads in Russia can imagine what a torture it was traveling to the hospital. Wolf and his driver carried me out of the transport and to the guardroom, which was also the reporting room. Wolf ordered the soldier on duty to summon a doctor, only to be told to be quiet, as it was the midday period. I saw red and bellowed, "Have you forgotten that there is a war on and people are being shot? Summon a doctor at once." A few minutes later a doctor appeared, put me on a stretcher, and wheeled me into the operating room. After I was cut free from my flying combination and boots, a doctor attended to my wounds. My knee and arm were X-rayed. As I lay on the operation table, the consultant surgeon introduced himself and said he had been the chief surgeon in the Junkers hospital in Dessau before he was enlisted into the army. He then divulged that a shell splinter lay under the kneecap, in the miniscus. There was also another splinter in my lower arm, and fifteen plastic splinters around my right eye. The removal of the splinter in my arm was no problem, the splinters around the eye must be cut out, but the operation on the knee would be a problem. There was the possibility that infection might occur, which could eventually cause amputation of the leg. An alternative was that he remove the splinter with instruments. I asked what chance of success there was of walking correctly after the operation, and he replied that a stiffness was to be expected, probably 20%. There could be only one answer for me. "Go ahead with the operation, doctor, I have complete trust in your ability." A nurse fitted the anesthetic mask and asked me to start counting backwards from 21. I counted and counted, then the doctor asked if I had taken anything since being wounded. I said yes and named the pain killer tablet I had taken. He then told the nurse to give more anesthetic, then I was gone.

As I slowly came to, I made out the faces of Bubi, Heinz, and Michel bent over me. I think we were all glad that we had cause for a small celebration. The doctor said that the operation had lasted six hours. In between there was a power failure and the emergency generator came into use. He believed that he had removed all traces of metal from the wounds. Instead of the usual plaster cast he had fitted a splint. Peace and quiet was the rule of the day, although a small movement of the knee was necessary to prevent stiffness. The doctor ordered a Krim-Tartar, who was a prisoner but worked in the hospital, as my personal helper. He was an exceptional person. He not only attended to my needs during the day, but slept on a mat by my bed. Should I want a drink during the night, or anything else, he was always at hand. I was given a telephone by my bed so that I could keep in contact with my comrades. I could ask them for things that were not available in the hospital. My wounds were healing quickly, and soon, after only 10 days since being wounded, I and other convalescent patients were flown in a Ju 52 over the Black sea, to the larger air force hospital at Bucharest.

A new commander, Major Freiherr von Bibra, took over my crew as I was in hospital. I could only advise them to seek their own way of avoiding it, while I intended to return to my unit as soon as possible. The doctor advised me to make sure that in Bucharest only the splint be used and not a plaster cast, as he was convinced that the healing process was better. We flew in an unheated Ju 52 over the sea at minus fifteen degrees celsius, and I lay on a strecher, as did other comrades.

From the airfield we were taken to the hospital in Sankas, and were laid out in rows in the entrance hall. We were given a blanket due to the cold, which I wrapped around me. On top of the blanket my uniform jacket with rank and medals had been laid. Then came a "God in white" to me and asked what I had. I became angry with his attitude and shouted, "I drove a train through the nursery, can`t you see what rank I have?" He checked my name and rank and said "Lieutenant, first of all you must take a bath, then a plaster cast will be applied to your knee." I threw the blanket off, and with my free hand, reached for my PPK pistol, which hung in my belt on the shelf above me. I told him that the doctor who operated on me made it clear that only a splint should be used and not a plaster cast. I drew my pistol and asked him if he was going to insist on his directions being followed. He then turned to a nurse and ordered that I be examined for lice, then washed and moved to room five.

As the nurse brought me to my room, I saw a large notice hanging over my bed which said "Danger. This patient shoots."

The matron, who was a nice young blond woman, came shyly into my room and asked why she had been warned about me. She shook with laughter as I related the performance in the entrance hall

In my room there were two other occupants; on my right was a lieutenant from an army mountain unit whose leg had been amputated above the knee. Against the wall opposite was a member of the Waffen SS who had lost both hands, his leg had been amputated, and he was blinded in one eye due to splinters. It was clear to me that I was lucky compared to these two. The next morning we were visited by the senior consultant with an entourage which included the chief doctor, two internees, the matron, and a nurse. They did not spend much time with the Waffen SS man, who was very apathetic and rarely spoke. The senior consultant doctor changed the purulent bandage on the other patient's wound without wearing protective rubber gloves. Then it was my turn, "Is this the man who knows better than we what is good for his health, or otherwise shoots," he asked. He removed the blanket which covered me and ripped off the plaster of the "window" on the splint, necessary for observation of the operated wound, which caused a jet of blood to shoot out of the wound. All this, incidentally, without washing his hands after changing the bandage of the other patient. I said quietly, "doctor, that was an incredible achievement." He looked perplexed, turned on his heel, and left the room with his escort in tow. From that moment on, not one doctor bothered with me. The matron, however, arranged that in a few days I could be moved to Germany, with the hospital train. My wound was healing fast, without a plaster cast. The journey took six days, during which I gently exercised my knee, within the splint, in small movements. I occupied a field stretcher on the third floor, so to speak. My thoughts turned to the other occupants in room five in the hospital. The Waffen SS man died one night. The man from the mountain unit knew, as well as I, what had happened. From his sad looking face, it was easy to see that he wished that he could come with me, but he was not able to be transported.

One can get used to a long six days journey. I had a view from the window near me of the scenery and railway stations as we passed through them. We made a long stop in Budapest where the train engine was changed and supplies taken on board. Water for the engine and for the carriages was also required. This all took considerable time. The same procedure happened in Vienna. Our train journey ended in Wuerzburg via Munich. Here the air force patients were off-loaded. A first-aid sergeant said we could choose in which hospital we wished to be, and when he called out the hospital's name, we should shout out. The first was the air force hospital, which could take 35 men. The second was the university clinic, 25 men. The third was a convent of the order "Serious Sisters," 2 men. I shouted straight away, "Here." I and another lieutenant were transported in an ambulance to the convent. Altogether, only ten patients were accommodated here. I was given a room for myself, and the Mother Superior appeared and asked me what preference I had for the midday meal. In a short time, there came pancakes with plumb jam, something I had long wished for. It was almost like being in paradise.

16

AFTER REST AND RECUPERATION, BACK TO THE FRONT

The third wartime Christmas I spent in the convent in Wuerzburg with the Sisters, who spared no effort to ensure the comfort of their patients. There was even a Christmas goose and genuine home baked biscuits and cakes. After Christmas I was visited by two comrades who were transferred from the squadron to the airfield at Giebelstadt as instructors. The airfield was near Wuerzburg, and on a high plateau above the valley of the river Main. As they saw how much my condition had improved, they promised to help me return to my home. On 30 December they appeared with an ambulance and an "order" to take me to Memmingen. In the meantime, I could get around with the aid of crutches. I changed into my uniform, complete except for the sports shoes I wore instead. First of all, they drove to a dance cafe in the town and carried me inside. There they wanted to make the aquaintance of two young ladies, with the forthcoming New Years party in mind. They thought that with me as an attraction they stood a better chance. They certainly attracted a lot of attention as they carried me into the cafe, and their plan to become aquainted with two young ladies was also successful.

My two comrades had previously bought train tickets for the journey to Memmingen, and informed the doctor at the airfield that I was to be met at the station and taken home. They put me in a second class compartment on the train. In Memmingen everything went according to plan. An ambulance and the doctor were waiting, and they drove me to my home at Memmingerberg.

Kaethe was overjoyed to see me, and although my daughter Ingrid hardly knew me, we soon became friends. Of course, my leg was a source of interest for her. The splint would soon be removed, and Ingrid helped in that she sat on my foot and bounced up and down when I sat on the couch. The doctor looked after my leg with competence. He arranged for me to be regularly transported to the airfield and back for the necessary therapy, which helped the healing process.

Kaethe did not seem to be overjoyed that we could be so long together during wartime, due to my wounds. I sometimes had the feeling that she would not be too upset when I had to return to my unit. Of course, she looked after me, so there were no complaints in that direction.

I was visited at the beginning of March by sergeants from the group, who came from Nikolajev in a Ju 52 to spend their leave with their families. I leared that the Ju 52 would be leaving the next day for the return journey to Nikolajew, with the post and other required items. They also informed me that my crew was waiting with impatience for my return. Until now they had resisted all efforts to detail them to other crews. As I could now walk with a stick and the doctor had no objections, I flew the next day to Nikolajev.

My return to the group was accompanied by enthusiastic greetings. During the winter flying had not been possible due to snow drifts, and later thaw weather turned the runway into a swamp, into which the aircraft wheels sank to the axle.

It was interesting to learn how the new pilot, Major von Bibra, coped with the flying aspect. The first attack was against shipping in the Black sea, to destroy the supply route to the Caucasus harbors. They flew in line until the crew detected a cargo ship, which was escorted by three fast gunboats. Von Bibra attacked in a steep glide and dropped the three 500 kg penetrating bombs, and then climbed and asked if we had hit the target. "No," was the decisive answer from Bubi, "the bombs dropped into the sea next to the ship. Our 1st Lieutenant Haeberlen does it better." There was silence during the rest of the flight. After we had landed, the major shouted to us, "Go to hell, I will decide what to do about you later." He never did do anything about us. Another aircraft's bombs had hit the target.

On the same day I flew a few times to see what my reaction was like after the operation. I found that everything was in order, with no problems, although I still had to use my stick. A few days later, one of the most well known bomber pilots, a Captain Werner Baumbach, was transferred to our group to fly with us against Russian ships in the Caucasus ports. In this field he had accumulated much experience from which we could learn. He had sunk more ships than any successful U-boat commander. Mainly his successes were between north of Norway, the Irish coast, and the north Atlantic. He attacked the escort and cargo ships on their way to Murmansk, which was the only ice-free port on Russia's Atlantic coast. He could be described as a well-built and handsome man. He possessed a certain charm which appealed to me. He was never high handed, and always friendly to us from the start.

On 24 March he commanded nine Ju 88s with experienced crews. The target was to be the harbor in Tuapse, on the east coast of the Black sea. It was one of the Russian navy bases in the Caucasus. Recconiasance had shown that a fleet of submarines, a large destroyer, two cargo ships, and frigates were anchored in the harbor. Each aircraft had a different type of bomb load. Baumbach decided that he would attack the submarines. We had loaded three 500 kg penatrating bombs and flew on his right wing, while Heinz Kunze flew on his left wing. We flew at a height of 16,000 ft. over the sea in an easterly direction. It was midday, and we thought that this would be a good time for a surprise attack, which proved to be true. As we moved into position for the attack, there was no anti-aircraft fire, although it was a clear day with no clouds and good visibility. Baumbach, who was in the lead, ordered the air brakes out. The other aircraft assumed attack positions on either side and behind him. We saw our target clearly as we dived. I had a large cargo ship in my sights. We could only release our bombs when the front aircraft had dropped his bombs. In the meantime the flack became active. As Baumbach's aircraft started to climb I had the target central in the bombsight. I let the bombs go, and with the air brakes in, climbed steeply in a long drawn out curve. I could see that most of the crews had made direct hits on the targets. Michel's photographs of the destroyed target were some of the best that he had taken. In spite of the heavy flack, we re-formed during the climb and landed after some four hours flight, mostly over the sea, without mishap. This attack on shipping was one of the group's most successful to date. Baumbach had sunk four submarines and damaged others. Two crews had direct hits on a destroyer, and we had direct hits on the cargo ship. In addition, the harbor buildings were also severly damaged. The reconnaissance later showed the cargo ship upside down in the harbor. A few weeks later, we again saw our photographs in the magazine "Illustrierter Beobachter." How this happened we never found out. That our lives were at risk in taking these photographs, and someone sitting comfortably at home collected the fee for them, was very annoying.

That evening in the mess we celebrated our success with red Krim wine. Baumbach was called to the telephone around 22:00 hrs, and I will never forget the ensuing conversation. We gathered that for the next midday, the same target would be attacked. Baumbach shouted in the handpiece "Colonel, doesn't anyone on the general staff have any idea of tactics? It is not a good idea to attack the same target on the following day. My children who play cops and robbers know more about tactics than you ever will." He then slammed the handpiece down. For the first time I heard the name Colonel Herhud von Rhoden, who had given the order for the attack. Through his stupidity he later caused a lot of trouble. In spite of Baumbach's disagreement, the order had to be carried out. We flew again at a height of 16,000 ft, but could see nothing due to the cloud which lay below us and over the target. The general staff also had incompetent meteorologists. By thin cloud we could just about see the harbor of Tuapse. Baumbach ordered a dive attack, and with the increased speed and at 6,000 ft we could see better. We looked for a target and dropped our bombs. We had to contend with flack, which was heavier than the day before. This time there was no surprise element, and the flack had started with our approach. We had hit more of the harbor buildings, but this was not a very successful operation. In an angry mood, Baumbach reported the results to the Division Headquarters and again spoke his mind. He was determined to complain to the general staff again. After Baumbach had flown successful operations with other crews, he left us. I met him some time later and asked how he had got on with his general staff meeting. He replied that he had been rejected. "They stand together," he said, "but for actual operations they haven't got the slightest idea."

A few days after the attacks on the Caucasus harbor and shipping, we were suddenly transferred to Odessa. There the group was to re-train on the latest aircraft, the Ju 88 A4. Improved engines increased the speed, and there was more crew protection with bullet proof metal and other improvements, all of which pleased the crews. We were accommodated in a disused sanitorium on the shore of the Black sea, which was a welcome change for all crews. We were given rotational leave and flew home.

I was promoted to captain on 1 April. Due to my being wounded and the long period in the homeland, Von Bibra gave me the command over the re-equipping of the group. Apart from the harbor, Odessa itself showed little damage. Rumanian troops were stationed here. Only a few German troops were to be seen who were here for a rest period. The life standard improved, since the front was several hundred miles away from us. My crew soon showed their ability in producing good meals. They obtained the supplies from villages in which only German settlers lived. The names were even German, such as Rastatt, Baden, and Karlsruhe. The settlers dated back to the time of Zaarina Catharine, who brought them to Russia to cultivate the rich land of Bessarabia. When one entered a village, one felt immediately at home. Everything was the same as in Germany. Farmhouses, churches, and even the badischen dialect was spoken. We exchanged our goods for theirs. After the war was lost, Stalin ordered that they be shipped to Siberia and Kasastan. This also applied to the German residents of the Volga republic.

At the beginning of May we flew without Michel, but with the chief mechanic, Heinrich Kratzert, to Memmingen in the old Ju 88 A3 to take delivery of the new Ju 88 A4. We had to fly back the next day, fully packed with supplies and mail. There was so much to pack in that I had the two transport pods fitted under the wings, where normally bombs were carried. Heavily loaded, we took off in the morning and headed for Odessa. It was usual with flights to the eastern front to land at Wiener-Neustadt. Since I had comrades there whom I knew well, I had informed them by telegraph before the flight that I would fly direct to Odessa. We flew at 6,000 ft above thick clouds eastwards and to the north of Vienna. Heinrich Kratzert came forward and sat between me and Heinz, and said "ola," which means "hallo." A spanish word he had learned when he was a member of the "Legion Condor" in Spain. "We have two good engines in our new aircraft," he remarked. No sooner had he said this, than a shudder went through the aircraft. The right hand engine came to a standstill, and we could see that a part of the camshaft protruded from the top of the engine. I feathered the propeller and ordered the jettison of the wing pods. I was busy trying to trim the heavily loaded aircraft, as Kratzert reported that because of the valuable contents, he had wire-locked the transport pods, which meant that they could not be jettisioned. In spite of full power to the left engine, the aircraft was dropping in height at some fifteen ft per second. We were busy looking for a suitable place to make an emergency landing, now that we were under the clouds. Where we were, we did not know, as we had, as was usual on long journeys, listened to music on radio Belgrade. Bubi made a couple of compass readings on radio transmitters, and after a quick computation, said that we were near Belgrade. In front of us was the Danube, and further forward was a railway line on which a train was traveling. Behind the train lines were poplar trees, and just beyond a plateau. I put the aircraft into a dive to gain speed and shot over the railway track and the trees. A few yards from the end of the plateau our nice new Ju hit the ground on the fuselage underside and came to rest in the field. Bubi had released the cabin canopy just before the "landing." "That was a close shave," remarked Heinz. Heinrich had noticed that I was not strapped in my seat, which was a bit thoughtless in the circumstances. He had positioned himself behind me and held the headset cable tightly in his hand so that I would not be thrown forward during the crash. He had helped me, but suffered injury to his knee, which made it difficult for him to move.

In a short while we were approached by a car. The uniformed Hungarian occupants turned out to be the police chief and the fire chief from Rokospaloti, the nearest town. They offered to help us, firstly by taking Heinrich to the hospital to be treated. After a while they returned with two other policemen who would guard the aircraft. Luckily, we had our washing kit stowed in the cabin. The rest of our kit was somewhere in the fuselage, where we could not get at it. With the promise to guard the machine day and night, they then drove us to the hospital, where we collected Heinrich, who had nothing seriously wrong with his knee, and took us to the Military attaché in Budapest, which was 20 miles away. At this time Hungary was still neutral. There were no German troops stationed there, but military vehicles had permission to travel through the land. The attaché was accommodated in a castle which stood on a hill above Budapest. It had an attractive view over the city. First of all, the nearest German airfield was contacted with regard to the salvaging of the aircraft. Next, our base was informed. We were given rooms in a hotel in the city, and pocket money for three days.

In the hotel I remembered that during our visits from Wiener-Neustadt to the Semmering and the hotel there, that one evening, in a good mood, I got to know a student who lived there. He had written his address in my diary, and said that if I was ever in Budapest again, I should visit him. The hotel porter found his telephone number and made the connection. At the same time I noticed that the porter stood at attention. I felt that something special was involved in the telephone call. The porter then told me that the Earl Esterhazy and family invited me to dine with them that evening, and that the young Earl would shortly be at the hotel. It was quite a surprise for me to see the student from the hotel in the Semmering. As we wanted to rest a little after our mishap, and above all take a bath, we did not talk too much. I explained that our suitcases were in the ruined aircraft, so we could only appear at dinner in uniform, and asked him to give our excuses to his father. We returned to our hotel rooms, tidied ourselves up, and rested for a while. At eight o'clock, a uniformed chauffeur called for us and drove us to an impressive villa with a long driveway. My crew were not so familiar with the ettiquite to be expected, so I told them to watch and copy what I did, in particular during dinner. We were escorted by a footman to the salon, from which one could see into the dining room. There was a richly decorated table laid out with three glasses and cutlery. The young Earl's parents greeted us so heartily that our shyness soon disappeared. Hungary, as a neutral land, lived in peace. The food was excellent, as were the different wines we drank, with Mokka and liqueur at the end. An experience of this kind was quite new to me. The young Earl drove us back to the hotel, with the promise that the next evening he would bring some friends and we would go to the Margarethen island. This was the well known amusement quarter of Budapest. It should be a very pleasant evening, during which we could make new aquaintances. The next day we visited the beautiful city of Budapest, where we saw not only the Parliament and the castle, but other places of interest, as well.

On the third day we received a message from the attaché that a team had arrived to salvage the aircraft. Great was our surprise when we got to the aircraft. In spite of the guards, everything had been stolen except our personal belongings, which were in the bomb bay. The thieves had dug a tunnel under the aircraft and had taken everything that was not screwed down. That evening we left on the night train via Vienna to Wiener-Neustadt, where another aircraft was waiting for us to fly to Odessa.

Heinrich Kratzert was sent on a long recuperation leave. In his place we had a soldier who was returning to the front after home leave. As soon as we wad started, Bubi and Heinz persuaded me to land at a military airfield in Budapest, since we were not allowed to land at civil airports. The landing needed all my concentration and expertise. All around the runway were trees and houses. The runway itself was only 2,500 ft long. In spite of this, the landing was successful. The two ran off to telephone a friend in the city, and they returned after a short time with large grins on their faces. They said we would shortly be collected by the father of Heinz's girl-friend. After a while, a chauffeur driven "Horch" arrived. This model car was on a par with a Mercedes and a Maybach, and a noble vehicle. The firm of Siemens in Hungary was represented with a Horch. We had only traveled a few hundred yards when there was a "bang" from the front of the car. After the driver had investigated the cause, he came to us and said that the left hand tire was punctured, whereupon I said "Gentlemen, it's a sign from heaven. We will start immediately for Odessa." The disappointment was very visible on the faces of my crew, but duty called. It was a difficult start on the short runway, but after two hours we landed at our base in Odessa. While we were away, new orders for the group's transfer to an airfield at Charkov had arrived, and two days later we were on our way there.

From 31 May to 20 June we flew 30 operations. I had completed 100 operations by 11 June, which brought a gold wings emblem for me to wear and a silver trophy for the crew. This was a special gift from Göring in recognition of proven crews. We made round the hour attacks on Russian supply routes, and now and again we attacked airfields which had aircraft on the ground. Many operations was the rule of the day. As adjutant, I had much to attend to, which meant that my crew had a day off now and again. On 1 July I returned after an operation, only to be told by the group's clerk that I was to be transferred, as Squadron Commander and instructor, to the group's instructional group. There, the newly arrived trainees from the homeland would be trained for the front. The IV./Bomber Group was stationed at Bobruisk, in White Russia. I received permission from my commander, Major von Bibra, to make a reconnaissance flight over the airfield at Bobruisk. It had been taken over by German troops without any damage ensuing. It was not far from the town, and while the parting from the group was depressing, I felt that one could live there for a while.

The reconnaissance aircraft in our group in Saporoschje was, at the same time as my transfer, disbanded, and the aircraft and crews were assimilated into the squadrons. Our comrades gave us a touching farewell party, at the end of which we were escorted to our aircraft as if in a burial parade. The technicians had produced a coffin with the inscription "Reconnaissance unit, rest in peace," which accompanied us in the "parade." As we took off, we could see the smoke and flames of the "dead" reconnaissance coffin. We had, as the fifth man, the indispensable technician, Hans. Haupt would drive my Ford V8 to the new unit. We flew over Kiev and the Pripjetsuempfe towards our new unit with a certain trepidation as to what we would find there.

17

TRANSFER TO IV./GROUP BOMBER WING 51, AT BOBRUISK

Up until now, we had only seen southern Russia. Now we flew from Charkov, which lies on the banks of the river Donez, in a northwest direction, past Kiev and the joining of the rivers Desna and Beresina, which later became the river Dnjepr. It flowed into the Black sea at Nikolajev.

The Beresina is a river with a history. Napoleon lost thousands of men trying to cross the river during his retreat from Russia after Moscow was in flames, including a contingent of enlisted men from Schwaben. Bobruisk also lies on the east bank of the Beresina, but somewhat higher. The airfield was captured without any resistance during the advance, so it was undamaged. The airfield, which was a mile and a half from the middle sized town of the same name, had a wooden runway, which was laid out in an east west direction. The accommodation was built for occupation during the winter, as well. The town showed hardly any signs of war damage. It had an attractive orthodox church, which had been turned into a brewery by the communists. In all other aspects, a typical White-Russian town, with the usual wooden houses on either side of broad streets. The road surface was constructed from cobblestones that were not exactly flat.

After reporting to Major Stemmler, my new commander, I was taken to my new squadron, number 10 Squadron. In the squadron headquarters I was given a room with a balcony. In an adjoining room there was a toilet and a bath, which only had a cold water tap. Hans and another aircraft mechanic constructed and installed a water heater. They built a double bottom in an oil-drum, which had a door through which fuel material could be fed, and there was a chimney through which the smoke escaped. Then a cold water pipe was fed to the bottom of the oil-drum, and at the top, an overflow pipe. The water could then be heated until it was warm enough for a bath. When the cold water tap was turned on, it drove the hot water into the bath. It was not long before all our bathrooms had this system built in. The Russian helpers were astounded at what the Germans could do.

The two other squadron commanders were Captain Vetter and Lieutenant Ali Berger, with whom I became quite friendly. He was killed in action on 27 Janurary 1943.

Sergeant Bernhard, the chief sergeant of the 10th squadron, and I had a good understanding right from the beginning as squadron commander. This lasted long after the war. He was a very reliable person who rarely took leave, because he felt that he was needed by his men. He finally went on leave after more than a year and found that his wife had a three month old baby. He could not understand that in accordance with the law, the child was his, although he was not the father. But then, after the war, he became reconciled with his wife, after a lot of persuasion by the commander, the doctor, and me. The war had brought a lot of unusual situations with it.

Apart from me there were only young lieutenants, complete with crews, in the squadron, and they had come direct from training schools. Their names were Lieutenants Czurusky, Haschke, Schneider, and Traeuptmann. They were given six weeks training in dive and glide bombing techniques, flying in formation, and attacks with live bombs on partisan areas. The army had requested our support when the partisans were in a good defensive position. To keep the army losses to a minimum, we bombed these positions, with success. We were fired on by light anti-aircraft guns, and machine guns which were specially constructed for defense against low flying aircraft. The partisans were led by experienced Russian army officers.

A special trainee was Lieutenant Dierich. He had been selected as a future commandant, and so received special training in dive and glide attacks, as well as firing in the air. Fritze Dierich was known to the elder officers as a flying instructor who commanded a flying training school. He compiled the air force duty system, which gave guidelines for internal organization and military duties. Flying subjects were, however, not included. In short, a smart looking Preusse who laid more emphasis on appearance and attitude than on flying a Ju 88.

My experience had led me to the conclusion that technical "know-how" and a feeling for flying were essential for the leadership of a Wing. The leader must, in all circumstances, be totally in control of his aircraft. Dierich had passed the course as aircraft leader, but he had not had the opportunity to gain any experience in formation flying. The aircraft leader must carefully judge the movements of his aircraft, so that the rest of the aircraft could follow in formation. This was important when a lot of flack was being thrown at the aircraft, or during attacks by fighters. Although I informed Commander Stemmler that, in my opinion, Lieutenant Dierich did not have the capability to be a unit leader, as he was quickly rushed through the training and transferred to Rostov within three weeks. There he took command of the I./ Group Bomber Wing "Edelweiss." Later I returned to my group as Squadron commander of the I Squadron, and found that he was my senior officer.

At this time, Bobruisk was several hundred miles behind the frontline. One could say that it was a "rest" town. There was a cinema which now and again showed a film. There was also a very attractive soldier's home and an amateur theatre.

Two large hospitals were also in the neighbourhood, in which Red-Cross nurses worked. In addition, there were other institutions, such as an army long distance telephone unit and an administrative unit, which organized the farming and what was left of other industries. There were also many women "helpers" from Germany that were nurses, news helpers, secretaries, and telephone operators. This was an obligatary duty.

Like everywhere in the east, in Bobruisk and the surrounding area there were, unfortunately, farming commissioners from the NS-Farming association in action. They wore a grandiose uniform, similar to that of the NS party in Germany. In addition, there were industry experts whose aim it was to get the industry back on its feet. They also wore impressive uniforms, but in the army colors, which they thought would lend weight to anything they said to the workers.

I had been in the squadron about ten days when a trainee lieutenant asked me if I was interested in spending an evening at the soldier's home in the town. He and others had been invited by Sister Maria, the mother superior. There would be other guests, as well. He finally talked me into it. Of course, the thought in the back of his mind was that I would drive them in my duty car.

At the soldier's home we were greeted by Sister Maria, who was a well-built and pleasant person to look at. In a nearby room were the other guests. One of them was a blond lady who was employed as a secretary. There was also a Battalion Commander from a unit of the Vlassov-Army, which, apart from German instructors, consisted mainly of Russian ex-prisoners who were against the communist regime and so had joined our side against the communists. Captain Holfeld was nearing thirty and had a pleasant personality. Later we often met, along with lieutenant Czurusky from Vienna and Paul Haschke from Bruenn, who joined the air force as soon as the Sudaten became part of the German Reich. Schneider and

Traeuptmann were also present. The blond lady sat between Haschke and Traeuptmann, while I sat opposite. As we were introduced, I was impressed by her. A spark had awakened in me.

It was an evening that would not be so easily forgotten, especially when Paule Haschke broke into song. He had a deep voice and sang with emotion, "Evenings in the Tavern." He was also reported missing after only a short operational period.

For me, the evening changed my life. I made intensive advances towards the only woman, other than Sister Maria, who was present at the party. It ended with me driving her home in my duty car. She lived near her place of work in a block built especially for German women who were obliged to work for the forces.

On the first evening available after my duties were completed, I drove to my blonde lady. After the soldier's home party, I had telephoned her and asked if we could meet again. I invited her to a horse race, which was to take place the following Sunday. In no time at all, I was spending all my free time with my new conquest, and Liesel was her name. She indicated that she was not adverse to my advances and that she favored me. The friendship soon developed into a deep love for one another, which exists to this day.

I was very surprised when in August I was ordered to attend the school for training formation leaders in Tours, France. On 21 August it was time to say goodbye to Bobruisk for two weeks. I started with my crew, and flew low over Liesel's place of work, as a farewell gesture.

After an in-between landing in Warsaw, we flew over Memmingen in a westerly direction. Bubi received a radio message that the airfield at Tours was enveloped in fog, so we could not land there. We flew instead to Orleans-Bricy, where we landed. A futher message after two hours gave the airfield at Tours free landing permission, but now there was thick fog over Orleans. I had long possessed a license which left the decision to fly or not up to me, independent of the weather situation. A duty car drove in front of us and guided us to the white line in the middle of the runway. It was the first time I had started under such conditions, but all went well. The visibility was between zero and 150 ft. I opened up the throttles and steered along the white line, which was just visable from the cockpit, and took-off blind. The chief instructor at the school was Colonel Dieter Peltz, a successful formation leader. He possessed the "Knights Cross with Oak Leaves and Sword," earned mostly from his successes against English warships. He had also sunk a battleship in a dive bombing attack. He had an extraordinary personality, together with a likeable charm. He behaved in the same manner to younger officers as he did to the older ones. On the course were also members from the Bomber Wing 51, such as Wilhelm Rath and Teddy Schwegler. My company chief from the war-school in Werder was also there, Captain Bischof. He said that I had achieved much, but we would see how I made out on this course.

In addition to the formation training school in Tours, there was also a school for training squadron leaders. Most of the trainees came direct from flying schools and had no front experience, nor were they prepared for air fighting. Our training consisted of air tactics and formation flying in enemy action, with lots of flying practice. Stress was laid on dive bombing practice and attacks in formation. After the training, every trainee had to dive-bomb a very small target. Bischof was quite disappointed to find that he was quite a bit behind me as far as the points scored were concerned. From thirty trainees, I and my crew came in third place in scoring points.

The officers' mess for trainees was in a castle which was near the airfield. It was situated in a large park. To this day, I can remember our last farewell evening. The meal was crowned by two hundredweight of lobster brought from the Atlantic coast. That was a meal not to be forgotten. Excellent French dry white wine flowed in an unbroken stream.

In our free time we had the oportunity to visit Tours. It was three miles away and was on the banks of the river Loire. Its cathedral is well known, and in the center there was an impressive square with a round fountain in the middle of which was a statue. The town suffered no destruction during the war due to the rapid advance of the German troops, and so was occupied without any fighting.

One evening we sat, with collar and tie, in a wine tavern with some of the town's "elite." They bet us that we did not have the courage to splash about naked in the fountain. It was twilight, and Captain Pfeiffer was the first to undress and jump into the fountain. He was the son of Professor Pfeiffer from the Goeppingen hospital. A neighbor, one could say.

Such meetings between the Germans and French were probably the beginning of the friendship which De Gaulle and Adenauer sought after the war.

The jump in the fountain was nothing compared to the "coup" which my crew, Bubi, Heiz, and Michel, played. In a dance cafe they got to know a corporal in an anti-aircraft unit. He turned out to be a well known orchestra leader in Berlin, Eberhard Bauschke. He sensed that due to the long period at the front, the three men had plenty of money. The money was in the form of credit certificates, issued by the German Reich, and these were valid in all occupied countries. Bauschke acted as band leader, and all three drank copiously, with the result that they were all drunk within a short time. A shuttle bus ran between the airfield and the town which gave the soldiers the oportunity to visit the town. A bus left the town at 01:00 hrs, and my three were on it, together with some young lieutenants from a parallel course. After a while, my three started to "sing" in a growling sort of voice our favourite song with the words "Where we belong, is in the air." One of the lieutenants remarked that the sergeants should shut up. This, of course, did not go down very well with Bubi. He made the bus driver stop the bus and shouted "Who do think you are, you young wipper-snappers. When three front fighters, grey from the propeller wind, sing, you should be quiet. So all of you leave the bus and walk the rest of the way to the airfield." It is hard to believe, but the young officers did just that. My three traveled to the airfield on the bus.

I had just got up one morning when the phone rang; I had to report to Colonal Peltz. He showed me a report from the young officers' instructor, regarding the incident on the bus. I requested time to talk with my crew, as I was not present at the scene and was rather surprised by it. I said I would deal with the situation. A very subdued crew stood before me and agreed with the report from the instructor. Peltz had threatened strong disciplinary action. On this note, I went to the officers' instructor and explained that they were an exceptionally good team who enjoyed operations and were very brave in serious situations. In addition, my radio operator possessed the "German Cross in Gold" and was one of the most recommended men of the unit. Almost on my knees, I pleaded him to withdraw the report, saying that the three would apologize in front of the assembled company. This he accepted. Three very dejected and white faced men stood before the assembled company and, one after the other, stammered their excuses, which I had formulated. They were well aware thet they had only just avoided a more serious punishment.

After a successful completion of the course, we flew back to Bobruisk on 3 September with in between stops in Memmingen and Lublin. Liesel was overjoyed to see me again. At the beginning of October, I was given two weeks home leave. This time I traveled by train, while Liesel during the same period would visit her mother in Berlin. In Brest-Litovsk we both had to undergo an unpleasant de-lousing procedure. Brest-Litovsk was also the railway point where the rail gauge changed from the Russian wide gauge norm to the European norm. Liesel was met in Berlin by an aquaintance who had arranged her job in Russia.

I spent a night at my godparent aunt's house in Babelsberg-Ufastadt, and the next day visited Liesel's mother, who lived in a wooden house in Britz that her nine children had built for her. The house had a small garden of which she was very proud. In spite of her age, she was tall and carried herself upright. From the beginning, I found her to be an exceptional woman.

After two days I said goodbye to Liesel at the railway station. She looked sad as I traveled further to my family.

There was nothing to hold me at home, but I now realized that true love was something quite different to that which existed between Kaethe and me. I was not angry, but felt more sorry for her, as I realized that she could never satisfy a man.

After a few days I visited my sister in Munich, from where I made many telephone calls to Liesel. I was pleased when the time came to jump on the night train to Berlin, where I would finally see Liesel again. Through her mother I got to know her brother, Wilhelm, who lived in Duisburg and was visiting his mother. He accompanied Liesel and me to the train that went to the front. As we took our seats, Wilhelm took from his watch chain a medal which he had received personally from Kaiser Wilhelm for good service as an official with the railway. He gave me the medal with the words "It will always bring you luck." "God protect you" came from his lips as the train started to move out of the station.

To this day I wear the medal. Once, after we had taken off for an attack, I missed my wallet, in which I kept the medal. I caused an engine to smoke and make unhealthly noises and returned to base. Actually, I was not superstitious, but two things were important to me. No flying without the medal, and no flying against the enemy on Friday the 13th.

The training of the continual intake of trainees kept me, as squadron commander, very busy.

The relationship between Liesel and myself became closer. I was determined to tie my future to hers and separate completely from Kaethe. A few days after this decision, Liesel confided to me that she was expecting my baby. I was naturally very happy, and felt that I was right in my decision.

One evening Liesel, Ali Berger, and a few lieutenants from the squadron were celebrating a pleasant evening with me in my room. We were all a little tipsy, when Ali suggested that we invite Commander Stemmler to join us. Liesel wore my white woolen cap that was my "trade mark" in both summer and winter in Russia. It was often pointed out to me by senior officers that I was "improperly dressed." This I ignored, since there were so few crews who had such high success in enemy operations. I felt that I could allow myself this derivation from the normal dress. We knocked on Stemmler's door, and without waiting for the customary "come in" opened the door and went into his room. He was soon persuaded to join us in our celebrations. We left him, but a short while later, he did indeed join us and celebrated, as well.

I was in the habit that, after the evening meal in the mess when Stemmler, as the oldest mess member, gave the sign that smoking was allowed, I did not join my comrades, but instead said my goodbyes and disappeared in the direction of the town. Stemmler took me to task on this matter and forbade me to drive to town in my duty car. The only alternative was to use a bicycle to visit Liesel, which I did. On the return journeys, at night, I was often fired upon by partisans but, luckily, never hit. Thereafter Stemmler allowed me to use the car. Now that he had met Liesel, he took every opportunity to play the "cavalier." I was not at all pleased with this development, especially when I returned to the front. It was not gentlemanly behavior for my senior officer.

There are two incidents which I will mention while I was at Bobruisk. My crew and I were on the way to our aircraft from the operations room. We passed by a working group of Russian prisoners who were repairing the road. As we neared the aircraft, we threw our cigarette buts away. Some of the prisoners scrambled for these. I took a full 20 packet of "Haus Neuerburg," my favorite brand, and threw them to the prisoners. On our return from the flight, I was informed in the operations room that I had to report to the airfield commander. One of the prisoners' guards had reported that I had given the prisioners a packet of cigarettes. "What do you think you are doing, giving cigarettes to these low-class people," shouted the Major of the reserve. "Sir," I said, "these prisoners are soldiers like me, doing their duty for their country. Do you want to be treated in the same manner if you are captured?" I saluted, turned on my heel, and left the room. He had also forbidden that the food leftovers from the kitchen be given to the prisoners. I could not understand his motives. In the nearby prison compound, we could see how badly the Russian prisioners were treated. Did not those who should know better understand that should we be shot down over enemy territory, how we would appreciate a cigarette? I was very indignant, but helpless.

There was also a unit which provided communications by long distance phone and teleprinter messages. The line to the unit which supplied our spares appeared to be out of order, so a repair troop, consisting of three men, was ordered out to locate the fault and make repairs. They were armed with pistols and rifles and left in the morning, but by evening had not returned. On the way they had made several reports that they had not discovered the fault. An army patrol then informed us that our repair troop had been massacred and laid out in a "Hakenkreuz" shape at the edge of a wood, on the road between Bobruisk and Mogilev. We informed Captain Holfeld, who with his men combed the area and searched the nearby villages. They found three Russians, one of whom was a regular army soldier. They had bazookas, Kalaschnikovs, and hand grenades. In no time at all a field court-marshal trial was convened. The judge and jury consisted of an army officer and a corporal.

"Death by hanging" was the sentence, which legally was correct and in accordance with the "Haager Land Fighting Regulations." This said that partisans and others who fought behind the lines, when caught, could be sentenced to death. This was agreed to by all Geneva Convention nations, except Russia. This is still valid today. Anyone who has not experienced the barbaric attacks of the Russian partisans behind the front line, whenever the opportunity presented itself, have no right to be critical. In general, it is these people who, of course, know better, and who cry for sanctions.

It was December, and winter was fast approaching. Just before Christmas I received my transfer to the number 2 squadron of the bomber wing 51 "Edelweiss" as Squadron Captain. On Christmas Eve we enjoyed an excellent goose dinner at Liesel's blockhouse flat. She did not eat much because she was sad at the forthcoming parting. I, on the other hand, managed in two hours to leave only the bones of the goose on the plate. In addition, a slice or two of bread, washed down with a bottle of French red wine. This, I felt, was the right "back stiffener" in view of what awaited me in the future. Sad, but putting a brave face on it, we said our goodbyes. I still, however, could not understand why I must leave at this particular time.

We were convinced that without our efforts, Germany would not be so successful. I know that this conviction to do one's duty, in the back of my mind, helped me a lot in later life.

As always we zoomed low over Liesel's place of work in an He 111, where she and her friends Hanni, Ria, and Hilde waved goodbye. I saw them waving for a long time, then I had an empty feeling, but I did not show how much the parting hurt me.

Slowly I came to realize that I now belonged to the 1st Group. There were new faces and comrades to get to know. It also occurred to me that Fritze Dierich in Rostov, where the 1st group was stationed, was my new commander. This was not a pleasant thought. After a routine flight over land, we landed at midday at our new operational unit at Rostov.

I had reported to Dierich and was on the way to 1 squadron when I was called to the telephone. At the other end was Liesel's sister, Lene, who worked in the telephone exchange. She had made the connection to Liesel in Bobruisk. Liesel now knew that I had arrived safely. Lene often made such connections, until she was transferred.

18

BACK TO THE FRONT WITH I./BOMBER GROUP 51

After several months away from the front, I had to feel my way back to operational flying. The comrades in the 1st group were unknown to me, apart from Dierich, who was, since October, the commander. I had to get used to new faces. Ali Berger was also transferred to the 1st group shortly after me, so there was at least one familiar face. He took over the 3rd squadron. Lieutenant Puttfarken led the 1st squadron, and before him Teddy Schwegler was the squadron leader. Puttfarken was most successful as a squadron leader. There were a couple soldiers in my 2nd squadron that I knew vaguely. A "Wastl" Winkel who was on Lieutenant Capesius' squadron in Bobruisk, and a technical officer for the group, Heinz Unrau. He was one of the longest serving members in the squadron.

Ali Berger and I were accommodated in a very small room in a building on the edge of the airfield. Against each wall were camp beds with small tables in between. If one sat on the bed, one could just about use the table to write a letter. Next to the door was a stove. A small window, which we could not open, let only a small amount of light into the room. We only slept and ate there, while my duties as squadron commander consumed a lot of time every day, as well as the operational flying requirements.

Two days after I had joined the group my crew and I were in operation. In the beginning we flew army support attacks against the Russian resistance strongholds, or Russian troops who were attacking our army positions. In the autumn of 1942, after the 6th army, which included Rumanian, Hungarian, and Italian contingents was surrounded weeks before in Stalingrad, the Russian army was attacking our forces who had advanced to the Volga river, and forcing them to retreat. They were too weak to hold the positions. Our task was to help the 6th army at their request, by flying attacks on specially selected targets. On 30 December we flew in line over the Kalmueck plain, close to the surrounding ring of Russians near Elista. Our task was to support General of the Artillery von Seydlitz-Kurzbach's troops, who found themselves in a precarious position. We successfully flew low attacks on tanks. That evening we received a message from the army saying that the cooperation between the army and air force was a success, and the advance of the enemy had been halted, for the time being.

We flew quite a few operations every day. It started early in the morning and continued until the evening. For the maintenance crews and armaments personnel it was a lot of work. For a long time we had frost to between minus 20° and minus 30° Celsius during the day. It needed a special knowlege and experience to start the engines in the morning. Hans, my mechanic, even sat in the aircraft all night, wrapped in furs, and every two hours started and ran the engines so that they did not freeze up. He was always sure that there would be no problems with the morning starts. He was extremly reliable, and because of this he accompanied me when I was transferred, which was a most unusual procedure. I did not want to be without him during operations. I have him to thank for an aircraft that was always serviceable. I followed the same procedure with my driver, Sergeant Haupt, who remained my driver as long as I remained on the squadron.

During my time as captain of the 2nd squadron we flew 104 missions against the enemy, between 27 December and 5 February. From this it is clear that, apart from the smooth running of the squadron, there was only sleep to think of.

As the Russian ring around Stalingrad closed, our 6th army was doomed. From the 120,000 troops, officers, and other ranks, some 120,000 ended as prisoners of war. 80,500 were killed. Others, such as the wounded, could be flown out. From the 120,000 Germans in captivity, only 6,000 were able to return to their homeland after ten years under horrible conditions in Russian prison camps. With the German 6th army, there were also Rumanian, Italian, and Hungarian soldiers who suffered the same fate (compare with author Paul Carell, "Stalingrad," Ullstein 1992, page 210).

The red army now advanced westwards, and the front came nearer. This meant that we did not have to fly so far on our troop support operations. At the end of December the flights took about two hours, but this time was reduced daily. The enemy continually moved west during night advances with tanks, motorized troops, armored cars, and mobile anti-aircraft guns. These could be hidden during the day-time in haystacks, under trees, and in the many farm buildings in the area.

On January 6 the Wing received the order to individually attack the advancing red army. The front line was 125 to 140 miles away in the east. After I landed from my fourth attack, a crew reported that they were damaged by flack some 20 miles from the airfield. I did not attach much importance to this, as the crews were inexperienced and I thought they had imagined it. However, after my return from my fifth attack, two other crews reported heavy flack only 20 miles away over a town with the name Semikarakovskaja, near Rostov. After I returned from my sixth attack, I decided I would take a look at the situation. We flew at a height of 120 ft over the main street of a typical Russian village, to the market square. Suddenly, flack burst all around us. I went into a dive to increase my speed and then climbed steeply in a curve. There was a horrible noise in the cockpit, and smoke appeared. The stick did not have any left or right effect. Heinz realized that the rudder was jammed and came into the cockpit to help. At not more than a height of 65 ft, the rudder became free and I was able to control the aircraft again. In the left wing was a large hole from a direct hit, which made control of the aircraft difficult. We were lucky in that, although the flack was heavy, we received no futher hits, and by flying low we escaped. After a lucky landing we inspected the damage. The flack had hit the wing between the inner and outer fuel tanks. There was a hole big enough for us all to climb in. No man could have greater luck. To prevent the "fear of flying" feeling, we took over a new aircraft, and early the next morning took off as usual.

At the briefing for the day's operations after this occurrence, I warned the crews of the danger of flying over Semikarakovskaja. I even pointed it out on the map. If one had to fly over the village, it should be at a great height.

At the time our Wing commander was Colonel Conrady. He flew with various crews, and he decided which one at the daily briefing. He flew as observer and must have been the last commander without any flying tuition. Once he flew with us instead of Heinz on a long flight at a height of 14,000 ft. We were to make a diving attack on troop and goods trains in a railway station behind the front line. I can see Conrady now; he was a very pleasant, uncomplicated person who wore a monacle at all times. He sat next to me and, despite the heavy flack bursting around us, did not seem to be in the least pertubed.

The next morning during the briefing, I again warned the crews about flying near Semikarakovskaja. On this day there was high-lying fog; the lower layers were at 700 ft, while the upper level was some 1,800 ft high. Conrady flew with the crew of Lieutenant Helm, who had gained experience flying against the enemy. We started two minutes after Helm's aircraft. We immediately climbed steeply through the clouds, and had just left the upper layers when we saw a large cloud from an explosion to the south of us. Bubi said "What idiot is flying over Semikarakovskaja?" since the explosion was in that area. The cloud from the explosion reached a height of more than 3,000 ft. After our return from the operation, we found that Helm and his crew, together with Colonel Conrady, had not returned. Helm had not taken my warning seriously. It was sad that we had lost our commander, a good crew, and an aircraft unnecessarily.

On 23 December Ali Berger and I sat opposite each other on our beds with the intention of writing long overdue letters and bringing our flight logs up to date. The stove in our room was lit earlier in the day by a Russian prisoner, and now burned well. Ali had flown more flights against the enemy than I had, and had achieved excellent results. The commander had recommended him for the "German Cross in gold" medal. "Klaus," he said, "in three weeks I am going on leave. I have flown over 300 operations, and in the next three weeks there will be thirty to forty more. That is more than enough. At home I will receive the "knights cross," which is long overdue, anyway. I think my parents will be very proud of me." I then told him that anyone in our position should not plan too far into the future. He just laughed at that.

The next day he flew a support mission for a Waffen SS tank division who was opposed by a more superior Russian tank force. He attacked in a low flying approach and received a flack hit in an engine, which put it out of action, and the aircraft became uncontrollable. He decided to make a forced landing in a field, but the aircraft exploded when it was almost on the ground. The observer and the radio operator were thrown clear, but Ali and his gunner were killed straight away. This was observed by Lieutenant Geruschke, who, without hesitating, lowered his undercarriage and flaps and landed between the enemy and the crashed aircraft in the field. He took the two survivors into his bomb bay and flew off. The Waffen SS had seen this and sent three of the newest type of tank on the front line, the "King Tiger," carrying soldiers, to the crash. They recovered the bodies of Ali and his gunner and arranged that they be transported to Rostov, where they would be buried. The soldiers who made the recovery were really brave. They had risked their lives to recover the crew, who had flown an attack to help them.

Fate could be cruel. The posthumous award of the Knights-Cross was no consolation for Ali's parents, as was the news that he had been promoted to captain. The whole squadron, together with all comrades, mourned him.

Ali's radio operator, sergeant Puls, who, after the war, lived with his family in Klosterlechfeld, had taken up a position as a civilian worker at the military airfield at Lagerlechfeld.

In the meanwhile, daily attacks were flown against enemy targets. Up to 30 January I had flown 200 operations. This was an occasion to be celebrated, but the situation did not allow it, since we had to concentrate with all that we had in order to relieve our surrounded army in Stalingrad. Without interval, we flew daily support operations. From the time in Rostov, two occasions remain in my mind, one pleasantly funny and one not so pleasant.

Back to Ali Berger. One time he was flying a mission with the aircraft flying in line. Two aircraft crews were straight from the training school. One of them had an engine failure. The other was ordered by Ali, over the radio, to return to base, and the one with the engine failure Ali ordered to fly next to him. Ali would fly on his left and behind him, and so guide him to the airfield, where he would make a wheels-up landing. We could see the two Ju 88s on their approach to the airfield. Ali was still behind the aircraft with the engine failure. We heard over the radio in the operations room the directions given by Ali, "Reduce speed, reduce height, lower flaps, and increase the intact engine revs." They were now over the runway, and Ali directed that the engine should be cut and to let the aircraft decrease speed on its own. The new man made a perfect wheels-up landing, and Ali, while he had fully concentrated on the landing of the other pilot, ended up in the same manner. His aircraft lay slightly behind and next to the other. An embarrassing situation for our best captain.

The second occasion ended in tragedy. The weather over Rostov was very bad. There was a high fog layer, with the lower level at 300 ft. This meant there was danger of ice forming on the aircraft, which could have disastrous results. The division ordered my squadron to attack troop concentrations near the village "X." I telephoned the divisional 1a, a Colonel Herhud von Rhoden, and explained that due to the weather situation only experienced pilots could fly the mission. I also said that I would send an experienced pilot with a meteorologist to make an assessment of the weather situation. Instead, he ordered me to fly and assess the weather in the target area. With the group's meteorologist I took off. At 250 ft ice started to form. The meteorologist became afraid and wanted to land. At full throttle I climbed through the clouds. As we came through the top layer, I saw that we had a lot of ice on the aircraft, but with the help of the anti-icing system it broke away, and with experience I knew that it would now thaw.

Above the fog's top layer cumulus cloud, I flew over the target area and, descending slowly, tried to see the ground. I was at 300 ft with still no sign of the ground, and the aircraft started to ice up again. We dropped our bombs—where, we did not know—and Bubi reported over the radio that there was too much low cloud over the target area, making an attack impossible. Starting and landing for inexperienced pilots would be fatal, and the division should be informed straight away. About an hour later we were again over our airfield, and the weather there had improved slightly. As we were on approach I saw that my squadron's aircraft were not there. After we landed, I went to the operations room, and was told that Colonel von Herhud had ordered the squadron to attack the target, although this was against my advice. I spoke to him on the telephone and said that three crews, which I named, would not return from the mission. Events were to prove me right. When the squadron returned after two hours, three crews were missing. That was twelve hopeful, inexperienced young men and three Ju 88 A4 aircraft, again, unnecessarily lost due to the wrong orders being issued by an incompetent staff officer. It was the same man who a year before had wanted to issue foolish orders before an attack on a Black sea port. He had never told what he had hoped to achieve with this. He was too much of a coward. Before the attack, I offered to take him with me to check the weather situation. This is just one example of the lack of responsibility of some members of the general staff, who issued orders without any idea of the effect they could have.

When we returned from a mission on 5 February I was surprised to learn that we were to be transferred to Saporoschje, where an advance party was already on the way. At the same time, notice was received that Fritze Dierich was to be transferred to a unit in Germany.

I was very pleased with the information that I was to assume command of the 1st group, the "Edelweiss Group" 51, which came at the same time Lieutenant Loeffelbein took over my squadron. He was, after the war, a state attorney in Giessen. On the very next day I flew on two operations, but then it was necessary that I attend to my duties as the new commander. This meant that my crew had nine days rest.

Also stationed in Saporoschje was the group's headquarters with its staff commanded by Major Kurt Egbert von Frankenberg and Proschlitz, who had been transferred from another unit to take over this command. We were the first unit to be equipped with the aircraft type He 177. Later, the only other unit equipped with the He 177 was also stationed at Saporoschje. In this aircraft, two engines were coupled together via a gearbox to one four bladed propeller. It proved to be a bad design. It would appear that Hitler had wanted an aircraft that could carry a large bomb load over long distances, with the intention of bombing the enemy's industrial areas far behind the front lines. The air force decision makers were, however, convinced that their ideas of dive bombing principles were better. The idea of a four engined heavy bomber was not considered. Professor Heinkel, a very pleasant mannered aircraft constructor, was given the order to produce an aircraft that was never used at front-line levels. In test flights, either a motor became overheated due to problems with the cooling, or a coupling shaft broke. An ideal request for a suitable aircraft was unnecessarily turned into a fiasco by people with fixed ideas. A complete waste of time and money.

Saporoschj was well known because of the large dam which lay to the west of the Volga. It dammed the river Donez, and the water driven generators delivered electricity to the industries in the Donez-Don area.

The Saporoschje airfield had many intact buildings and was the largest operational base that I knew of. The possibility existed for experienced pilots to carry a greater bomb and ammunition load, so long as the distance to the target did not require fully fueled tanks.

February 17th saw us in action again, this time against advancing Russian tank groups. Two days later my crew and I came up against a ticklish situation, which we duly overcame. As we were in a shallow dive to increase speed to make an attack on an enemy column, there was a loud explosion, and the cabin filled with smoke. Michel cried into the microphone, "The tailplane is breaking away, and there's a large hole in the fuselage." In the rear vision mirror I saw that the tail was in a strange attitude, bent over to the right, but it had not broken away. We thought we had been hit by flack. Slowly, and with utmost caution, we came back to our airfield, where we landed normally and taxied to our dispersal. Our Ju presented a somewhat strange sight. Hans climbed into the aircraft's rear to see what further damage had been done, in addition to the large hole and the "bent" tailplane. He let out a surprised cry and came out of the aircraft. In his hand he held the remains of one of our bomb's detonators, which had become unscrewed. Normally it was activated by an electrical impulse when the bomb was dropped, but in this case it seems it was set off by the vibrations from nearby flack explosions. A similar situation never occurred again. My crew were shocked, but I made it clear to them that Hans would make a new aircraft ready for take-off, and within an hour we would fly in the next operation. I made my report in the operations room and had something to eat. Then it was time to go to our new aircraft, which was always kept ready for me as commander, since it was known that I would fly as many operations as possible. I was of the opinion, as squadron leader and now as commander, that I would not ask of the personnel under me anything that I myself would not undertake. I came to our aircraft and asked Hans where my crew was. They had told Hans that they would not fly any more today, and he thought they would be drunk by now. I ordered him to go quickly to their barracks and tell them that if they did not come straightway, I would find me a new crew. A few minutes later they arrived somewhat sheepishly at the aircraft. It was obvious that they had had one or two beers.

Bubi was, however, capable of operating the radio. Michel was on the border-line, but Heinz had drunk a couple of beers too many. After we had started, we hung the oxygen mask on him so he could breathe pure oxygen for a while, which would help to sober him up. On this mission I did not need Heinz anyway. The target was near the previous one, where we had only nearly avoided a catastrophe. I knew through experience that after a shock, it was better to fly again, straight away. Otherwise one "bottled up" the feeling after a dangerous experience, which could lead to complications.

During the night of 21-22 February, I was awakened by my most experienced aircraft captain, Sergeant Schultheiss, who said that the Russians were coming. "Between 20 and 25 large tanks are advancing in our direction, and they are only ten miles away." While I knew that the Russians made advances with tanks during the night, I had ordered that a crew fly periodically over the Saporoschje area and drop parachute flares. It was clear to me, after this report, that the Russian advance was directed to capture the dam near Saporoschje. I alerted the whole airfield with our alarm system. I then telephoned the general-staff officer responsible for the army that was stationed in Saporoschje, and informed him of the observations of my reconnaissance flights. He laughed and did not believe me. I could now hear firing from our 8.8 mm anti-aircraft guns that were positioned around the airfield. When these guns were in the correct position, they were very effective against tanks. The Russian tanks withdrew to cover after the first salvo. I asked the staff officer on the telephone, "can't you hear the guns firing? If it was not for the air force the Russians would be on the dam." With that, I hung up and dressed quickly, and ordered all mechanics, armorers, and others to pack a minimum of necessary articles and go to the aircraft dispersals. There I explained the current position, with the possibility of being overrun. If the situation deteriorated and we had to vacate the airfield, all the group's ground personnel would be flown out in the Ju 88s. To this end I ordered that all aircraft be made at least serviceable to fly.

The order to attack a railway station behind the front line the next day that was 125 miles away was received from headquarters during the evening of 21 February. Under the circumstances, I disregarded the order and ordered that all Ju aircraft capable of carrying a bomb load be loaded with penetrating and fragmentation bombs. We knew the latter from our low level attacks at the beginning of the offensive. This time we could drop them from high altitude. At six o'clock in the morning the ground crews began loading the aircraft with the required bombs. In the meantime, the group was on alert. Even the sleeping army was now aware of the Russian advance. By flying in the area where Schulteiss had first detected the enemy, I was able to make out badly camouflaged tanks. I flew at 100 ft over the area for an hour, in order to see if other groups of tanks were visible. I could not detect any enemy troop or tank groups. I flew seven attacks on the enemy tank positions during the afternoon. By evening they were all damaged or destroyed. We then were given the order to attack the advancing enemy tanks, which we had already done.

The dam was saved. My troops had heard that the provisions store in Saporoschje had been deserted by the soldiers who, in fear of the advancing Russians, had made their way over the dam and fled in a westerly direction. There followed a regular procession of our lorries between the airfield and the deserted store. All manner of good things to eat and drink ended up in our store. A few days after the danger was past and the front was again 100 miles away, there appeared a high ranking army officer who demanded the return of the supplies. In view of this, I spoke with the commanding general of the air force, General Pflugbeil, explained the situation to him, and requested his intervention with the army so that we could keep the supplies. This was achieved, and we retained the supplies.

A very brave action can be attributed to my adjutant, Lieutenant Wastl Winkel. His comrade, the squadron's technical officer, 2nd Lieutenant Geruschke had flack hits in both engines and made a belly landing not far from the Russian tanks. Wastl knew that Geruschke had rescued two of Ali's crew not so long ago. Without further thought, he turned, lowered the undercarriage, and landed next to the crashed aircraft. There was no thought given to the landing situation; there could have been holes or other obstacles in the way which could have meant that he would crash. His crew opened the bomb-bay, and the aircraft rolled next to the crashed aircraft, from which the crew hastily jumped. With full throttle Winkel steered towards the Russian tanks and was just able to lift above them. He climbed in a steep curve without being hit by the flack and returned with eight unwounded men. As I heard of this episode, I telephoned the adjutant at staff headquarters and suggested that for his part in the rescue, Wastl should be awarded the German Cross in Gold to be presented in front of the whole group. The adjutant then told me that recommendations for the awarding of higher medals must travel via the usual channels.

Once more I was made aware that "Saint Bureaucracy" was the master, even during wartime.

The next morning we—that is, myself, Captain (Med) Dr. Denkhaus with his camera, Wastl Winkel, Geruschke, who was the intelligence officer, Lieutenant Oeberg, and the 1a, Alfred Fritsch, who had come to me from the III Group—drove in the duty car to see the results of our attacks on the Russian tanks. We also learned that the Russian general who had organized the attack had been killed by a bomb splinter from a 500 kg bomb which exploded near the hut in which he was studying a map. This, of course, made quite a difference to the course of the Russian attack.

This happened during our first air attack on the tanks. There were many tanks destroyed by bombs, and countless destroyed vehicles strewn over the area. As we looked closer, we saw, to our surprise, that the tanks were of American origin, and instructions on the dashboard were in English. This was the first evidence that military supplies were being delivered from America to Russia. These were shipped via Murmansk, Russia's only ice-free port on the Atlantic that, due to the Gulf-Stream, did not freeze over in winter. We knew from Baumbach that continual transport columns came from Murmansk, carrying supplies to Russian units. As a member of the bomber group 30, the "Eagle Squadron," he had flown many missions from Norway over the North Sea and attacked the shipping there. He had sunk many freighters and escort ships.

We learned three days before the attempted Russian break-through that we in Saporoschje would receive a visit from the chief of the armed forces, Adolf Hitler. We later referred to him, cynically, as the "The best war-lord of all times." This came about due to direct orders from him which caused heavy losses, for example, Stalingrad. As the FW 200 Condor, a four engined passenger aircraft, was landing, I drove in my Ford V 8—which had accompanied me since Paris—to where Hitler would arrive, wanting to see for myself how the proceedings would progress. On the way I met General Pflugbeil, who was in a duty car instead of his large camouflaged Mercedes. He looked at me with a flabbergasted expression and said "Haeberlen, how can you appear in that car now that the Führer has landed? You must not be seen here in such a car." As I left the area, I saw Field-Marshall Manstein arrive, as well as other high-ranking officers, all in duty cars and not in their usual large luxurious cars. I was at a loss to understand this. Why shouldn't we, who risked our lives, drive around in large confiscated cars.

A few days later, an incident occurred for which I was responsible. When returning from a formation attack on the enemy, I, as usual, came down to a height of 1,800 ft and ended the formation, whereupon the aircraft dived steeply in a curve and prepared to land. But this time I turned sharply, lowered the undercarriage and flaps, and prepared to land. Bubi reported that behind us was Ju 52, which I had "cut off." In the rear view mirror I saw with trepidation, that the Ju 52 was only about 1,500 yards behind us. Not only that, Bubi suddenly said that a flag flew on the small mast which protruded from the cockpit. This denoted that a high ranking officer was on board, and I saw more trouble ahead. We did not know who was on board, but I taxied faster than usual to our dispersal. We had just left the aircraft when a Mercedes SSK roared at high speed towards us. The Major-General von Richthofen climbed out and demanded to see the pilot responsible for the maneuver during the landing approach. Without hesitation I went to him and stated my position, rank, and name, and that we had just returned from an attack on the enemy. "Captain," he said, "I want to see the pilot who had the cheek to cut me off on my approach." "I must apologize, General, it was me. I did not know that it was the general's aircraft." I had a feeling that a very black cloud hung over me and that a cloudburst was inevitable. "You are a bad example to your men, which is not acceptable. I will consider what punishment is suitable." He then went to my aircraft, which was in the process of being re-armed and bombed up. "How many kilos of bombs can your Ju 88 carry," he asked. "2,250 kg, general," I answered, to which he exclaimed that this was very unusual. I then explained that if the target to be attacked was not too far away, I could carry less fuel and more bombs. "Apart from which, I am the only one in the group to do this, while the runway is not the best." "Very interesting, captain," he said as he climbed into his car and left. After the next operation, I entered the mess, where a large number of officers were gathered. I felt that something was in the "wind," but could not put my finger on it. A short while later a mess steward handed me a teleprinter message, which came from staff headquarters. As I read the message I turned white. It read, "Captain Haeberlen is immediately transferred to the airfield at Poltawa as the company commander of the airport personnel." It was signed by von Richthofen. It was like a slap in the face, especially since he had congratulated me regarding the extra bomb load that I could carry. The officers in the mess had gathered around me. One said that the whole thing was a "gag" thought up by the "higher-ups" to teach me a lesson. I had often been confused by orders from command that made no sense. "Gentlemen, I have learned my lesson, now let us drink a beer or two." As our stores were full, thanks to my clever flight sergeants and the intervention of command, the flow of beer and wine was assured.

For a change, we had at least one pleasant day in Saporoschje, on the occasion of the presentation of the Knights Cross medal to Flight Sergeant Spieth, an excellent pilot who, with his crew, had flown more than 200 successful missions against the enemy. He came from Ebersbach, which was not too far from my home. General Pflugbeil made the presentation personally in the presence of the whole Group.

Apart from the usual daily operations against airfields, railway stations, and in support of our ground troops who suddenly found themselves in a critical situation, nothing unusual happened over which I can write. Just one thing occurs to me. On 28 February we were returning from an attack when our right hand engine failed. We had to fly some 95 miles over enemy territory on one engine until we reached our lines. I climbed slowly without using the full power of the remaining engine. Should enemy fighters attack us, we had some reserve which might get us out of danger. We were lucky in that we were not attacked, except for heavy firing from encircled Russian troops that we flew over. I achieved a normal landing, with one engine and lowered undercarriage. Similar situations were an everyday occurrence during our operations.

As well as the flying operations, I had, as commander, much to do in the wing's office. I left a lot of the work to my reliable staff. There were, naturally, some things that I must personally deal with One such instance was when a flight sergeant returned from home leave with the problem that his wife had had a baby, although he had not been on leave for over eighteen months. How could I advise him? I did not have much life experience, since I was still in my younger years. I could only refer him to our doctor, who was older and possessed more experience with which to deal with such a problem.

Returning from a mission, I found that the group was to be transferred to an airfield at Bagerovo, which lay on the east point of the Krim. Again, everything was packed for the move to an unknown airfield. I asked the wing commander for permission to take two days off, which I needed to fly two officers from 1V. Group, who were transferred, to Brobruisk and bring two comrades back to Bagerovo. I had the opportunity to see Liesel again, and we spent a few pleasant hours together before the return flight.

The move took place on 2 April. It was a large airfield, with a long runway. We saw the docks in the town of Kertsch, which we had bombed in 1942 before the Krim fell into our hands. This part of the Krim was not settled, and there were no villages or farms in the area. A few Krim-Tartars who were friendly towards us, as they did not like the Russian communists, moved around in the area. After the war, Stalin had them moved to Siberia, where they were never heard of again.

Accommodation for the aircrews and technical personnel was in buildings that were in an acceptable state. Others had to make do with bunkers. At the beginning of our time in Bagerovo, I was driving in my duty car from Kertsch to the airfield when, typical for the area, I got bogged down in mud. Luckily, there came from a nearby pioneer group an all-purpose tractor driven by a corporal from Bavaria. He duly pulled me out of the mud, for which I thanked him. He then said in his broad Bavarian dialect that the Krim was at the end of the world, but Bagerovo was in a hole in it. He had really hit the nail on the head.

We had been moved to Bagerovo to support the withdrawal of our troops from the Caucasus and the Kalmuecken areas. Russian soldiers had gathered opposite the Krim, on the Asian side of the Black Sea's west coast. Here were the important harbors of Novorosisk and Tuapse, which we had successfully bombed in the first few months of the year. They were also on the northwest coast of the Asov lake as far as the town of Asov, where the river Don flows into the sea. The towns to the east—Krasnodar, Armavir, and Maikop—were again in Russian hands. Our missions, therefore, would require that we fly over the sea. Before our attacks began, we had a few days rest. We spent some of the time visiting the Feodosia harbor and the well-known Bakschiseraya monastery, which was in the hills beyond the "Krim Riviera." Later the famous three "war-lords," Roosevelt, Churchill, and Stalin, who were no better than Hitler, decided the future of Europe in Yalta, which was on the Krim Riviera. The scenery there is really pleasant, with palm trees and olive trees in abundance.

On 11 April we commenced our army support attacks, in that we attacked Russian artillery positions and supply routes, as well as motorized groups. My crew and I flew, from Bagerovo, altogether twenty missions. On 17 April I started on my 300th flight against the enemy. Of course, this was an occasion for celebration with my crew and other comrades. On 16 April we were given the task of a long distance attack on the oil fields in the Grosny area. The oil fields were situated on an old army road which lay beyond Maikop on the north border of the Caucasus. In addition to 1,500 kg high explosive bombs we carried five large flares. An extra fuel tank was also fitted. Heinz had, as usual, worked out the course, and slowly we climbed in an east-southeast direction. After a while I asked Heinz if our course was not too near the town of Krasnodar, and while there we could expect intensive flack. Shortly after we were caught in several searchlights. We were a flying target directly over Krasnodar. As always on a long flight, the automatic compass was steering the aircraft. I switched it out and flew sharp curves to the right and to the left, while at the same time I increased and decreased height. It was almost like airfield show flying, although we were hampered by the load we carried. At such moments one loses all sense of time, and there was no knowledge of how long one fought for life. Thereafter, there was no conversation for a long time. Slowly and carefully we climbed to 9,500 ft. In spite of the good weather the orientation was difficult, but we found the old army road. I flew lower and dropped the first flare so that we could see better. Then the weather suddenly changed for the worse, and to the east was thick cloud.

In the meantime our extra fuel tank was empty, so I jettisoned it. We circled the area in the clouds, but could not make out the target. There suddenly appeared a gap in the clouds below us, and we dropped two flares and in their light we saw the army road clearly. There was a lot of traffic movement, amongst which we could see tankers. We decided to attack them straight away instead of flying to our original target, since we did not want to use more fuel in circling that was necessary for the return journey. I again flew over the gap in the clouds, dropped the last flare, and in a sharp curve dived and dropped our bombs. We knew we had scored hits, because we saw large fires break out under the slight cloud. After more than four hours flying we landed back at Bagerovo, then after a short pause we took off again in the afternoon to fly support attacks for our forces. In the next two days we flew eleven sorties supporting our retreating troops.

On our return from the last attack on 18 April, there was again an order for our transfer, this time to Poltavo. The next day I flew there to see how my group could be accommodated. On arrival I was pleased to meet an ex-trainee of mine, Hogeweg, who was now a captain and squadron leader in a bomber squadron. He was highly decorated with the "Knights Cross" with oak leaves. This he received for exceptional results during attacks on Russian airfields and railways carrying supplies. I had feared that it would be a problem to accommodate all of my group. In conversation with command, however, I learned that it would only be for a short time, since we had been selected for a special task.

In Poltava, with the aid of the airfield commander, whom I knew, I was able to fill my Ju wing pods with supplies that were difficult to come by in the Krim, as the supply lines were continually disrupted by enemy action. The return flight proved to be somewhat hazardous. At about 5,000 ft over the Asovsch sea, our left hand engine suddenly failed. I immediately feathered the propeller. "I'm sorry, comrades, but we have to jettison the supplies in the pods, otherwise, we will end up in the water." In a very small voice, Michel said that in order to secure the pods, he had wire-locked them. This meant that they could not be jettisoned. Without delay, Bubi gave out an S.O.S. on the radio to alarm the sea rescue teams, who with Dornier seaplanes were active in the Black sea and the Asovsch sea. They would be starting and would fly to the position we had given over the radio. With the remaining engine at full power, I endeavored to maintain height. To this end I jettisioned quite a lot of fuel, but kept enough for the rest of our return flight. Heinz, who was searching the horizon, suddenly said that the Krim coast was in sight. We were now only at 100 ft and had flown over the last hill before the runway, when we saw a dust cloud below us caused by a complete Wing taking off and coming in our direction.

I was forced to make a steep right climb so that the other aircraft could fly past us on our left. For the landing I was forced to ignore one of the basic rules of flying, in that I made a sharp turn over the dead engine to avoid landing on uneven ground. Then everything followed very quickly. Undercarriage lowered, flaps lowered and, to increase speed, dropping nearer the ground. A steep left curve, and behold, our Ju sat on the ground. I was very relieved. I could imagine what the other pilots would say, such as "Don't you know that it is fatal to make a turn in the direction of your dead engine?" I, of course, knew this, so I had gained enough height and speed to enable me to throttle down the right engine. We did not want to fall on our faces, as it were.

One day my commander, Kurt Egbert von Frankenberg and Proschlitz, interested himself in my private affairs. He said that it had been reported to him that I had a close liaison with a lady news gatherer, although I was married. "This is not worthy of an officer, and further, not allowed." My short answer ended the conversation abruptly. "Major, the lady in question is not a news gatherer, but a secretary who carries out her duties in my office."

I had been expecting something along these lines due to my past experiences with him. When we were in Saporoschje he inspected, on the spur of the moment, the accommodations of my group. As fate would have it, he entered the room where my crew were resting. They lay comfortably on their beds in accordance with my instructions, which were that all the group's personnel should take no notice when anyone with a higher rank entered their room. Of this, of course, the commander was unaware. This meant that no-one shouted "Attention" as he entered, and all present stood up. "Why is there no military order," he wanted to know. Bubi, being the eldest, said that Captain Haeberlen had said that military order did not count as long as the crews were on duty. "Hmm!" was the only utterance from the commander, who left the room and made his way back to the squadron headquarters. As group leader I was summoned to appear before him. He said that I commanded a band of hooligans and not a military disciplined squad. "Major," I said, "would you please check and see which of the groups under your command have had the most airworthy aircraft available for operations." Upon which, I was dismissed. Two days later I was again summoned to his presence, where he said that much to his astonishment, my group had 20% more aircraft available than any other group. In this case, he retracted his complaint. I wondered if he now believed that, as I had found in my experience, that special effort is not achieved through pressure, but through trust and comradeship, up to a specific point, especially during wartime. This major was eventually taken prisoner by the Russians. Ten days later he was heard on a Russian propaganda radio station saying that it was better to defect to the other side and work in a peaceful socialist climate, rather than die for a criminal cause. He was in East Germany after the war, under Ulbrecht, one of the originators of the "National Committee for Free Germany." He was also a founding member of the "Federal German Officers" in Russia. Both organizations were communist oriented. In these organizations were also German ex-prisoners of war who were, for propaganda purposes, against their country and ex comrades, with, of course, the thought of better conditions uppermost.

They were and still are, for me, men without any character whatsoever.

Field Marshal Paulus was, to my way of thinking, also without any character. He was too cowardly to order a break-out of the 6th army while he still had a chance. That was at the end of 1942. A complete and experienced army sat still in Stalingrad. Of course, Paulus would have appeared before a court-marshal for disobeying an order. The result is debatable, but would probably have ended with the death sentence, and Paulus would have been shot. This was the penalty for acting independently in a specific situation, which was probably not appreciated by the higher command. An example is the action of General Yorck who, in 1812 at the Convention of Tauroggen, stated his case. He had, apparently, not only acted on his own authority, but acted in a traitorous manner. He wrote to the King, and stated his case in a dignified manner, with full knowledge of the consequences:

"Your Majesty knows me as a quiet, rather cold man, as long as everything goes according to plan. When this is so, every true man accepts this as his duty. But the circumstances had changed, and I was in a completely different situation from that planned. I await impatiently the reply from your majesty as to whether I should advance on the enemy (Napoleon) or the heated political situation condemn me. Your majesty, I swear that I would calmly die from a bullet on the sand, as from a bullet from the enemy. (Compare H.J. Schoeps, Preussen, "Pictures and Evidence" Berlin o.J., page 27f).

Another character failure of Paulus, was that he did not surrender the complete army to the Russians, although what remained of the once proud 6th army was a mass of hungry and depressed men. He became a prisoner with his baton in his hand, leaving Major-General Strecker with his X1 army corps to carry on fighting until 2 February.

Only one general did, in the circumstances, what he had to, and that was Lieutenant-General von Hartmann, who commanded the 71st (Niedersachsen) Infantry division. He fought the Russians with a rifle in his hand until he was hit.

Major Kurt Egbert von Frankenberg and Proschlitz, later, in the DDR, filled the position of "Military Commentator" with the East-German radio. He was also the organizer of the DDR Motor sport club, which was an imitation of the West-German ADAC. He had left his family to fend for themselves in West Germany. He then was given a divorce and married a colleague. As an excuse for these actions, he wrote a book with the title "My decision." It had in the introduction, "Memories of the Second World War," and "The Fighters for the Free Germany Movement." My brother-in-law sent me this book. He was a member of the SPD, which was automatically a part of the SED. He was disappointed in the "True Socialist" system, and so criticized it. This led to his being sent to the West as a pensioner. He died a convinced member of the FDP, whom he believed followed a national liberal policy.

In 1994, before the government elections, Kurt Egbert von etc, etc, was a candidate for the PDS.

After the group moved to Poltava, nothing special occurred. We could rest and recuperate before we moved on 6t May to the Illesheim airfield near the town of Bad Windsheim, in Germany. It was also a large park for aircraft. It had been decided that we would be trained on the new fighter, the Me 410. This aircraft had special weapons to combat the American B-17 four engine bomber known as the "Flying Fortress," which, due to its defensive weapons, was very difficult to attack. They flew in large numbers over Germany. We awaited the future with trepidation.

19

TRAINING IN THE ME 410 IN ILLESHEIM

It was a fundamental change for us to again be in our homeland after so long in Russia. At last we had suitable accommodations, a passable mess, and we were looking forward to going on leave in a short while. My first directive was that during the training, all married men had the possibility to be with their wives as long as they could find suitable accommodations in the area. There was enough time in the next months for the group to regain our bodily reserves and prepare ourselves for operations in the future. My flight log for this period contained flights all over Germany and the occupied countries.

I had to visit staff headquarters in Brjansk, whereby I had the opportunity to visit Liesel. My ex-adjutant, 2nd Lieutenant Wastl Winkel, flew as my wing man. He flew so near to me that in curves our wing tips overlapped. He watched my body movements, and thus knew what I was going to do next. We were greeted with applause by the company, to which Liesel belonged.

I was sent to Tours for a few days to learn fighter tactics. This was something completely new to us.

Our Ju 88 A4 aircraft were sent to groups in Russia, or to flying schools. The conversion also required that technicians attend courses for new equipment. The new Me 410 was a two-seater aircraft, for pilot and radio operator, which meant that crews who had flown, and fought, together for years must now be split up. Many were trained as pilots, but were never in action, because before their training was over, the war ended. Heinz and Michel were not attached to another crew, but also entered the training school for pilots. The final parting, after much danger, but also many good times, was not easy. One good thing was that the whole group had survived the war.

On 19 June there was a meeting of all group commanders in Brjansk. I flew on the morning of June 18th in an He 111 to Bobruisk, and on the next day further to Brjansk. The meeting had been ordered by the commander, Major Heise, and was held in the operations room. I was from the 1st Group, next to me was Major Voss from the 2nd Group, and also Wilhelm Rath from the 3rd Group and Captain Schoelss from the 4th Group. During the evening, as we sat over a glass of wine, Heise received a telephone call to the effect that Russian aircraft were approaching. As we knew from past experience that these annoying attacks usually did no damage, we remained seated with our glasses in hand and continued our conversation. We heard a couple of explosions, and the report came that the aircraft had departed. Suddenly, very near to us, we heard a crashing noise. Someone went to investigate the source of the noise and returned looking very pale, and said that we should all come to the stairway. About halfway up the stone stairs lay a Russian 50 kg bomb. From the end of the bomb came a hissing noise and smoke. We all returned quickly and called a bomb disposal expert. At first we thought the bomb had a delayed fuse, but the expert said, after he had made checks, that the bomb was a "dud." We had, once again, been lucky. Shortly thereafter, the news came that my He 111 had received a direct hit from a bomb. The bomb seemed to also be of bad quality, since there was an entrance hole in the top of the left wing and a hole in the underside about six feet square. The workshop chief inspected the wing and said that nothing essential had been damaged. He could make a temporary repair, which would enable me to fly back to Illesheim the next day. But once there, the wing should be replaced.

During her pregnancy, my Liesel was examined and controlled by competent doctors in the hospital. It was also an advantage that one of the doctors was a gynecologist. He had advised her only to return to her parents' home in Berlin after the birth of the child, while almost every night there were air attacks, which caused considerable disruption. I visited Liesel after my return from Brjansk, and the doctor, who was making his rounds, had also just arrived. As he heard that I would be flying to Illesheim the next day in an He 111, he asked me if I could take, as passenger, Liesel, while here there could arise complications which would be better handled in a hospital in the homeland. I was, to be honest, somewhat flabbergasted by the suddenness of the request. I said that I would consider it during the evening and let him know my decision in the morning. To influence me positively, the doctor had also said he would let someone who could deal with any medical problem that might arise fly with me. I now had a problem, in that I had previously agreed to take as passengers two sergeants who were going on leave. The aircraft was also loaded with boxes of ham and beef and a few hundredweight of onions, which were in short supply in Illesheim. The comrades in supply had asked me to bring these things. After much thought and without discussing it with anyone, I came to a decision. At about 3 o'clock in the morning of the next day, I would fly Liesel, one of the sergeants, and the man that the doctor had recommended to Illesheim. The other sergeant must wait for the next opportunity to fly out. I informed Liesel and the doctor that they should be at the airfield guard room at 2 o'clock in the morning.

My radio-operator was Sergeant Puls. He was a survivor of the shot down aircraft of Ali Berger. In air-traffic control, I gave the number of passengers who were to fly with me in the He 111, and requested that the runway lighting not be switched on. A white spot lamp at the further end of the runway was all that was necessary. The weather was 8/8 cloud cover, not too promising. The tops of the hills around Illesheim were reported to be in the clouds. Liesel was given the usual flying helmet and headset. She then had to climb over onion sacks and boxes to enable her to reach the flight-deck, where she sat next to me in the observer's seat. An airport car brought us to the aircraft. For the first time since I flew the He 111, I adjusted the hydraulic pilot's seat higher, so that I could see better during take-off with the heavily loaded aircraft. At 0:55 hours I opened the throttles, and with the usual racing pulse which I always had during take-offs, we lifted off. I had kept the aircraft on the ground until the last moment so as to increase speed for the take-off. To the east the first faint rays of the rising sun could be seen, while to the west there was only thick cloud visible.

I selected wheels up and positioned my seat in the normal position for flight, and we climbed slowly through the clouds to about 7,000 ft. This was the first time that Liesel had flown. After I had steered to the course required for Illesheim, I switched on the automatic pilot and Puls selected the radio the station from the army transmitter in Belgrade, which was transmitting music. Now we could breathe freely, as there were only the instruments to keep an eye on. Puls said that we had just overflown Baranovicze, which was previously on the border between Russia and Poland. The sun came up over the clouds to the east, and the air was calm. After about three hours flying, I noted that the oil temperature indicator of the right hand engine was too high, and thick oil was showing on the engine cowling. I had no other choice than to switch off the engine, feather the propeller, and give full throttle to the left engine in order to maintain height. From the start we had flown above the clouds. "Puls, where are we?" I asked. "Give me the course to Breslau." I had roughly worked out that we must be south of Breslau. The experienced Puls gave me our position after a few minutes, and it was some 30 miles from Prag. Puls made contact with an air force airfield in Prag-Rusin and was given a course thereof. I changed course, and we headed for Rusin. We learned that the weather there consisted of thick cloud down to a height of 200 to 300 meters, and the hills around the airfield were partially in cloud. I was aware that I could not fly further on only one engine with a heavily laden aircraft and decided to land at Rusin. It was not possible to make a normal blind landing. I had to try to fly directly to the runway, so Puls gave me constantly updated course changes, and when I felt that we were near enough I dropped steeply through the clouds. It was a question of my often practiced blind-landings combined with the experience of Puls as to whether we would successfully land or not. I never gave a thought to failure. The altimeter showed 600, 500, 400, then 350 meters, and we were below the clouds. The runway was directly in front of us. With undercarriage lowered and flaps out, we made a gentle landing. I was much relieved, which can be well understood. I taxied to the hangar in which repairs were being carried out, but I had forgotten that here there was no war activity and things were done by the "book." Liesel needed urgently to visit the "little girl's room," so her escort, detailed by the doctor, went with her to find a toilet in the hangar. I made my way to the control tower to arrange the repair of the engine. It was all so quiet compared with a forward airfield nearer the war zone. I saw from the tower that mechanics were already working on the engine. I presented the flying order to the sergeant and said "Clearance straight away for a flight to Illesheim." The sergeant said that I must first report to the meteorological office to be given permission to fly. I said "Give me clearance," and laid my authority to start when I wished before him. After some consideration, the sergeant said that he could not give me clearance, as I had a female on board. He then mentioned that this was against regulations, so he could not give me clearance. I would have to seek permission to start from the airfield commander, Lieutenant-Colonel Von Treskow. "Connect me immediately," I ordered. I was told that the commander was not on duty. "Give me the telephone number and I will personally ring him. "Von Treskow" said a sleepy voice on the other end of the line. I explained the situation and added that it was a medical emergency. I also added that I would fly further in any case, with or without permission, as soon as the engine was repaired. He then said I should telephone the Air-Ministry and obtain permission to start from them. No sooner said than done. The sleepy voice of the duty officer on the other end said "Here is Major Haserl, what can I do for you?" It was immediately obvious to me that he was an Austrian. I explained the situation once again and mentioned the difficulties I was up against. To my relief he said that I should continue with my flight, and von Treskow should make a report regarding the occurrence. Further, he also said that when I arrived in Illesheim I should make a detailed report to the Air-

Ministry. I thanked him and said it was a pleasure to deal with responsible officers like him. I then informed Lieutenant-Colonel von Treskow that I had received permission to start from the Ministry.

In the meantime, my engine had passed the tests required after repair. The oil-feed pipe flange had become separated from the engine, which accounted for the oil loss.

At 08:10 hrs we took off and set course for Illesheim. I climbed through the clouds to a height of 7,000 ft where the air was calm. Puls contacted Illesheim by radio, and they asked if anything had happened that necessitated my return from Russia in the middle of the night. I merely said that Puls should say that the commander had important matters to attend to. I then asked for a weather report for the airfield. It had improved so much that I was able to fly the last few miles without instruments. Although I made a soft landing, the He 111 suddenly got a bad jolt since the runway was not even. This was unpleasant for the passengers. I let the aircraft roll to the end of the runway and shut down the engines. Haupt appeared with my car. Liesel sat next to him and wore my white uniform cap. I gave instructions to the effect that he should drive Liesel and her medical escort to my accommodations in the barracks, which also housed other group officers. This was outside the guardroom. As I arrived on foot a few minutes later, a few comrades, looking rather surprised, asked me if I had not just driven with Haupt to my quarter. "As you can see, you are mistaken," I said. I confided in one or two of the older officers, but apart from my crew and Haupt, no one else knew that Liesel was with me. Once in my quarter, I asked the group's doctor, Denkhaus, to visit me and asked him to arrange transportation to the railway station in Nuernberg for Liesel and myself. From there we would travel to Munich, where our child would be born in a maternity clinic. In the meantime, I persuaded Liesel to type, at my dictation, my report to the duty officer at the air ministry regarding the flight from Bobruisk to Illesheim. Liesel's medical escort was going on leave to Berlin, and I asked him if he would deliver my report to the duty officer at the air ministry.

Doctor Denkhaus had arranged for an ambulance to take us to the railway station in Nuernberg. There we said goodbye to the medical escort. Liesel and I caught the train to Munich, where we were met by my brother-in-law, Kurt Ziegler. Due to an amputated leg, he was allowed to drive a private car during wartime. He had lost his leg in a flying accident in a W 34. The next day Liesel entered the clinic.

In the meantime, we had received directions as to how the conversion to the Me 410 would be carried out, as well as the re-training of the crews to fighter aircraft. From July onwards, the crews were to be first trained in Memmingen on the Me 110, including air to air firing. This meant that the pilot had to "aim" his aircraft at the target. It was a completely different technique from dive bombing a target on the ground. In the time in between, I commuted between Memmingen and Illesheim, with occasional diversions to Riem, Munich's airport. Our daughter was born in the clinic in Munich on 30 July. We had decided that we would name her Dagmar.

I learned that on 26 July I would receive the "Knight's Cross" medal, presented by the commander, Major Heise, in Illesheim, before the complete group. I can still remember the following celebration in the mess with my comrades, few of whom survived the war.

On the following day my crew and I, together with Hans, drove to Geislingen, where the town had planned a reception for us. On the morning of 4 July 1943, we were escorted, from my parent's house, by dignitaries of the town and party. The five of us, my parents included, were each escorted by a highly placed dignitary. The others and I—myself by the mayor—were escorted through the lines of the Hitler Youth and the Association of Young Women, to the town hall, where a march past of the complete Hitler Youth of my home town took place. Later, in the Town Hall, a celebration was held, and I was granted the honorary citizenship of the town of Geislingen-on-the-Steige. In a short speech, I thanked everyone involved in the preparations, and the mayor, for the reception and the honor I had received. I especially thanked my crew and our technician, Hans Seiderer, who with their untiring devotion contributed to our welfare and safety. And, of course, I thanked the whole group, the 1./ K.G. 51. In the town's Golden Book, I wrote a well known passage from Schiller, which effectively said that one should be prepared to offer one's life for his country, otherwise one could not win.

At that time I could not imagine that this honorary citizenship would be, for whatever reason, taken from me. This happened at the end of the war. The reason given by the mayor's office was that the Americans had ordered it as they took over the town. This I saw as another lie given out by the German authorities, while the Americans handled enemy soldiers correctly, unless they had performed offenses against the rights of man. In my home, two water color paintings of my hometown hang on the wall. On the rear is the dedication from the mayor, "You can be certain of the thanks of the German people." These are, in today's bureaucratic dictatorship, just empty words.

It seems that money and a comfortable life are more important than the love of the country. This attitude can contribute to the downfall of the state, since the basic rules have lost their value.

After our return to the group, I was occupied with the retraining on the Me 410. At the beginning of August, a teleprinter message arrived which read that I must report to the G.d.K (General of the air force bombers), who was the responsible officer in the air ministry for all bomber units in the air force. Accompanied by my adjutant Winkel, we flew over Leipzig to Rangsdorf. Liesel had in the meantime moved in with her sister in Leipzig because Berlin was bombed every night.

The newly appointed G.d.K was Lieutenant Colonel Werner Baumbach with whom we had flown successful attacks on shipping in the Black sea. I reported to Baumbach alone. He greeted me in a friendly manner and came straight to the point. "It has been reported to me that on 24 June on your return journey from Bobruisk you had, without permission, a woman passenger on board. This, as you know, is strictly against regulations." I explained the situation, including my relationship with the woman in question. Baumbach laughed, and said that as far as he was concerned the matter was closed. I then asked to know the name of the person who had reported me, while those who knew about it were reliable people. He said that he did not know who it was and that it did not matter to him, anyway. He further added that I not only showed courage during attacks, but also in other regions. Later in the mess we discussed other matters over a drink or two.

Much later I found out who had "shopped" me. It was the sergeant who was going on leave that I could not take with me on the flight. The real reason, however, was revenge. This sergeant was an armaments technician, who had been with the K.G. 51 since 1937. I could recommend, as commander, suitable sergeants from crews for officer training. As this became known, he reported to me and asked if he had the necessary qualifications for an officer, to which I replied in the affirmative. "I'll tell you soon to which crew I've allotted you, as gunner. Then you can fly a few times in action. Afterwards I will recommend you for officer training." He answered that he had not thought of flying in action, whereupon I said in that case, that I would not recommend him and dismissed him. I think I acted correctly, since comrades with such a character I would not accept as officers in my unit.

At the beginning of August we collected the first Me 410 from the factory in Augsburg, and the training started in earnest. Actually, the new aircraft was no more difficult to fly than our old friend the Ju 88 A4. Even so, with the first flying training, we lost one of the best pilots, Sergeant Schultheiss, who had first seen the advance of the Russian tanks in Saporoschje. On approach, he did not have enough air speed, and his aircraft suddenly fell to one side, hit the ground vertically, and burst into flames. We had lost a comrade who, for a moment, had failed to concentrate.

A squadron captain was seconded to the group to train us in the new tactics involved in air firing. The crew now consisted only of the pilot and radio operator. He could not train us in experience, however, with regard to the armaments of the aircraft. These consisted of two rocket launchers under each wing and two machine guns in the nose. We were to engage the American B-17s, which flew in a tight defensive formation. The plan was to split up the formation so that individual aircraft could be attacked. The theory was sound, but how that would function in practice, no one knew. In practice flights I tested the climbing ability of the Me 410 and the ceiling with a full load, with particular attention to the height at which the B-17s flew. As it did not matter what route we flew on these training flights, I often flew evenings to Leipzig-Mockau or Schkeuditz. During every flight I made exact notes on the aircraft's performance.

I could now and again see Liesel and our daughter, Dagmar. I started early in the morning so that at the start of duty, I was back in Illesheim. Bubi seemed to enjoy flying with me, and arranged that as soon as I arrived we could take off. After a further two weeks continual performance practice flying, I wrote a letter, via the G.d.K. in the air ministry, to the technical department. I explained my doubts as to the feasibility of the plan and gave my reasons. The B-17 had four engines, each with 1,200 hp, and two high altitude superchargers. The Americans could use their superchargers at 10,000 and 20,000 ft, thus maintaining the full power of their engines. Our Me 410, however, had two engines, each with 1,750 hp, and one high altitude supercharger which was brought into play at 10,000 ft. This meant that when we were at 20,000 ft altitude we had only half the power of our engines. How could we successfully attack when our Me 410 was "sluggish" to maneuver and slow? My conclusion was that with this disadvantage, an attack with rockets would not be successful. I never received an acknowledgment from the air ministry.

In the middle of August we were given notice that we would soon be transferred to Hoerrsching, near Linz on the river Donau. This would enable us to attack the B-17s which came over the Alps from southern Italy. At the beginning of September the training was completed, and the Me 410s were ready for action.

With some tension and curiosity, we waited for orders for the first operation.

20

UNSUCCESSFUL MISSIONS WITH THE ME 410 AND RELIEVED OF MY COMMAND

We did not have long to wait for the first operation. On 6 September we were given the order to attack a formation of B-17s consisting of 240 aircraft. The name "Flying Fortress" was very apt. Each aircraft had ten double machine guns, caliber 13 mm. Their target appeared to be the Bosch factory in Stuttgart.

We started with seven Me 410s and flew west. Despite their climbing ability, we had only reached a height of 17,000 ft as we flew over Stuttgart, and we witnessed the enemy aircraft drop their bombs on the target. As fast as possible we tried to catch up with them so that we could attack. I decided we would climb, which would give us a slight advantage, and we could fire our rockets into the formation. As I had written in my letter to the air ministry, our engine power was now so much reduced that we could not get nearer than 3,500 ft to the now home flying aircraft. Just before Nancy we came within range. "We will try to attack" I said to Bubi, and pointed our aircraft downwards towards the formation to enable us to fire our rockets.

What then happened, we will never forget. We were used to flack from the ground bursting around us, but what burst around us was like uncountable colorful fireworks. Bubi said that we were mad. Such concentrated defensive fire we had never seen. There was now no return, the only thing we could do was to close our eyes, fire the rockets, and dive steeply. Where our rockets went we could not see. all we could see was heavy defensive fire from the formation, aimed in our direction. At a height of 16,000 ft I leveled out and saw the closely packed formation, as if controlled by a ghostly hand, flying west.

I now had time to consider the rest of the squadron. How had they come through this first action against the flying fortress formation? Not too well, it would seem. Although they were experienced men who had many unpleasant flying experiences behind them, this must have been something quite new, and shocking. After about two hours we landed in Illesheim, only to find that a crew had landed before us. Shortly afterwards, two other Me 410s landed. We waited and waited, but three aircraft of my group did not return. We waited anxiously to see who reported. Lieutenant Hovestadt's aircraft was badly hit, and he and his radio operator baled out. Unfortunately, he landed in a tree and badly injured his leg. He was crippled for the rest of his life. The other crews were also caught in the defensive fire, which killed two radio operators. The first operation with new weapons was a shattering experience for us. My report of our experiences contained my conclusion of the new air defense idea. But, as usual, no responsible person at the air ministry took any notice of it, let alone did anything about it.

We were put on a 24 hour alarm readiness, but due to mismanagement of the "powers that be," we had not received the necessary ammunition for the aircraft machine guns from the supply unit. It was a Saturday morning, and I gave my 1a, 2nd Lieutenant Alfred Fritsch, the directive to organize the delivery of the ammunition straight away. It was obvious that without the ammunition we could not fly in action. The air force munitions depot was not too far away from the airfield, so Alfred sent two armaments sergeants to the depot to collect the necessary ammunition. They returned empty handed, because they did not have the necessary permission from the appropriate authority. My adjutant, who in civil life was a commercial school director, telephoned the authorities in Wiesbaden and demanded to be connected with the quartermaster. The voice on the phone said "Here is general so-and-so, why are you ringing us?" "This is 2nd Lieutenant Fritsch, the 1a of the 1/ K.G. 51. I would like to request authority be given to draw the necessary ammunition from the munitions depot, so that we can carry out our orders for the readiness of our Me 410s." To which the reply came, "Don't you know that it is Saturday and after duty hours? It is just by chance that I am here." Alfred shouted into the phone, "This is ridiculous, Saturday or not, today is for four years wartime, and we need the ammunition." The general replied that the person responsible for the issue of ammunition could not be contacted. Alfred decided to act on his own initiative, and with the two sergeants went to the munitions depot, armed with rifles and pistols. There, unbelievably, despite the protests of the guards, they obtained the necessary ammunition. That this was possible during wartime was unheard of!

A few days after our disastrous first attack on the B-17s, we were transferred to Hoerrsching, near Linz, on the river Donau in Austria. It was quite a large airfield, which made it possible to position the squadrons effectively, in that when the alarm sounded, at least one squadron was in a favorable position to take off, with regard to the wind direction. Unfortunately, during a training practice we lost three aircraft, but no lives were lost. During take-off, a formation leader veered to the left and crashed into the next aircraft, and into these wrecks crashed another aircraft. This had consequences, in that the divisional commander looked for someone to blame. As is usual with "Preussen," it was the commander.

I had become ill with sinusitis. Our doctor forbade me to fly at heights, which meant that I was unfit for action. I cannot remember the exact day, but it was at the end of September. The alarm was given, and an attack ordered. The B-17s were heading for the Messerschmitt factory in Wiener-Neustadt and were to be attacked by us. My stand-in was an ex-student of mine in Bobruisk, 2nd Lieutenant Merlau. He had flown many difficult operations and was an excellent formation pilot. After the disaster over Stuttgart, we had given thought as to how we could best attack the B-17s. We had decided that we would fire our rockets at the formation in a frontal attack and then dive so as to avoid the defensive fire. We calculated how big a silhouette of a B-17 should be in our sights so that we could determine when to fire.

Merlau attacked the B-17s at a height of 20,000 ft from the front, but was hit in the eye by a bullet that came through the canopy. He was immediately blinded in this eye, and a natural reaction was that he swerved, followed by the rest of the formation, and so lost height. Some aircraft attempted to climb, but without success. The Me 410 was just not capable of attacking the B-17s. The aircraft landed one after the other in Hoerrsching. We would just have to wait until the air force "powers that be" came to the same conclusion as we.

With short notice I was, on 11 October, ordered to proceed to Vels on the Wagram, which was not too far from the well-known Melk monastery, situated above the Danube. I must attend an important and secret information discussion. The meeting was attended by myself, and my new adjutant Lieutenant Pape (Wastl Winkel would shortly be taking over a squadron). I flew through the very scenic Donau valley, past Melk, to the airfield at Vels on the Wagram. There we learned that Reichsmarschall Göring would be present. He was visiting all defensive airfields, one after the other, and was expected to land in about half an hour to inspect the two fighter groups consisting of Me 109s and Focke-Wulf Fw 190s. They were also in action against the B-17s, which were increasing the number of their attacks. The pilots of these groups were already on the parade ground as we arrived. I met General Froelich, an Austrian who, shortly after the annexation of Austria, came to us in Memmingen to gain experience with our air force. I came to know him well. As the oldest officer present, I took station on the right wing of the parade. The two group's commanders were captains. I was given my promotion to major on 1 October.

The special Ju 52 landed, and the Reichsmarschall of the air force, Göring, left the aircraft via specially constructed steps to take his weight, followed by his entourage consisting of many officers. He came to the parade, whereby I reported "Sir, Major Haeberlen, commander of the 1. K./G. 51 with the fighter groups J.G. 7 and 10 on parade." His first question was "How many B-17 aircraft have you shot down?" To which my answer was "None, sir." He turned to his technical officer, Major P.C. Neumann, and asked him if I was the man who wrote the report about his experiences with the Me 410. The major said yes. The Reichsmarschall then told me that Germany possessed the best aircraft in the world. My answer was that this was propaganda, and we at the front knew better. He then "flipped out" and, red faced, shouted to us that were all cowards, and if we could not direct a squadron he would demote us all. Without a further glance, he went further along the lines and always asked the same question, "How many B-17s have you shot down?" I stood there as if carved out of stone and feeling deeply hurt. Then, Major General Bruno Loerzer came to me. He was a comrade of Göring's during the first world war and was now the chief of the personnel department, responsible for leadership. He said that I should not be so depressed, the Reichsmarschall was in a bad mood today. I answered that the Reichsmarschall's insulting behavior to a front line fighter was something one did not expect. "My trust in the capabilities of the air ministry chiefs of staff no longer exists. If it isn't possible to recognize the true position in the air, then we can't fight the war effectively." In the meantime, Göring had reached my adjutant Pape, who was a slightly built person. He asked the usual question, and received the usual answer, though Pape added that he was my adjutant. He was then given, completely unexpectedly, a jab from the marshal's rather large baton, which caused him to stagger backwards.

"My god" he said when he came to me, as Göring with his trail of officers headed for the mess, where a second breakfast awaited them. "Is that the thanks for over 200 missions on the Russian front, if that is so then they can all kiss my arse." With tears in his eyes, this brave youngster stood before me, completely bewildered by the behavior of his superior officer, the Reichsmarschall. One officer who wanted to console us was pushed roughly aside by Göring. It was the commander flying for the air space in which we operated, Major Handrick, an Olympic winner in the 1936 Olympics. He saw, however, that we had had enough and would not listen to him anyway.

Pape, with our camera man, who had flown with us to record everything on film, was about to report our return flight to the tower when we heard that all pilots and officers must assemble in the operations room to hear a speech given by the Reichsmarschall. In the room stood a desk and rows of chairs. The commanders and squadron leaders of the two groups and Pape and myself sat in the front row. There then appeared Göring's chief adjutant, Major von Brauchitsch, whom I knew from my two previous meetings with Göring. He saw me and said that I should sit at the rear so that Göring would not "flip out" again when he saw me. Again insulted, I sat in the last row between a lance-corporal and a corporal, both of whom wore the German Cross medal in gold. Then came the "fat one" with his baton. He was resplendent in a very light blue shiny uniform, with the orders "Pour le Merite" and the "E.K. 1 and 2" from the first war. He also wore an order, "The large cross of the knights cross, " which was a "show-off" order made specially for him. He made himself a laughing figure with his flair for overdoing things. After a few introductory words, during which he explained to the front line fighters why the German people were forced to fight the war, was the sentence, "If I was not loved so much by the people, I would climb into a fighter aircraft and destroy the enemy." The corporal sitting next to me said rather loudly, "Arsehole," which said everything.

Before we flew back to Hoerrsching, I said to Pape that he should arrange that all the group's officers should assemble in the mess, as I wanted to explain the day's events. Then our He 111 should be made available to fly, as I must be in the divisional headquarters to report to the commander, Major von Buelow, to give him a run-down of the day's happenings. After we landed, I gave a short account of the proceedings to the officers in the mess and added that a coward stood before them, so called by our Reichsmarschall. After reporting to the division's commander, I would apply for leave, then wait and see what happened. Sergeant Papenfuss, one of my best pilots, flew me to Schleissheim, where the divisional commander's car was waiting for me. The driver drove me to Major von Buelow's office. He was also active during the first war as a fighter pilot and wore the "Pour le Merite" medal. He had already heard of Göring's difference of opinion with me and wanted to hear my version. I explained briefly the gist of our conversation, whereupon he said that all the personnel who worked for Göring were pigs in his eyes, as he himself was. "He concerns himself more with his collection of European art for his house in Karinhall than with his air force, who now find themselves technically worse off than the enemy. But now we will drink a special brew," and he opened a bottle of champagne. He explained many things to me that I would not have thought possible during the evening, during which we emptied three bottles. He was later also involved with the group responsible for the assassination attack on Hitler, on 20 July 1944. "Your wife is in Munich, so go and join her and wait until a fighter pilot is needed."

In a drunken state, I drove to my sister's flat in Munich-Bogenhausen, where Liesel and Dagmar were. My sister had moved to our parents' home in Geislingen to avoid the nightly air raids. With the words "you see a coward before you," I greeted Liesel and went to bed.

During the next few days I tried to relax. I was pleased to be with Dagmar and hoped to be left in peace for a few days. It was not to be. During the third night the doorbell rang and rang. In pajamas I opened the door to find a corporal and a sergeant from the field-police with large metal badges on their chests, which were a sign of their absolute authority over all ranks of the army. "We have to escort the major to headquarters in Berchtesgaden. It is an order from the air ministry general staff." I answered to the effect that as I was in bed when they came, they should come again in the morning at 07:00 hrs and closed the door. They left without a word. Exactly at 07:00 hrs I left with my escort, who drove me to Schleissheim, where by an Me 108 was my group commander, Major Heise, waiting. With a stern expression on his face he said that he was very disappointed in me in that yesterday I had cast a blot on the honor of the bomber pilots. That was another blow to me, since I had not expected this. In fact, I was convinced that my comrades would be on my side, as all I had done was to tell Göring the truth. Without saying a word, I sat next to him and we flew to the Ainring airfield, Hitler's airfield when he visited his main headquarters in Obersalzberg. Göring had, with a small staff, taken up residence there.

After we landed, I was taken to a room in the flight operations building and told to wait. Heise flew back to Schleissheim without a further word to me. After about half an hour, two officers appeared; one was von Brauchitsch, the chief adjutant to Göring, and the other was Dieter Peltz, who was once "General of the Bomber pilots," whom I knew from my pilot training in Tours. Von Brauchitsch had a sheet of paper in his hand. I stood up and to attention. He read from the paper that on the order from the Reichsmarschall of the air force, Hermann Göring, I must give the following order:

Major Haeberlen, commander of the 1. K.G. 51 is, with immediate effect, relieved of his command. As the result of exhaustion and the following nervous reaction, he can no longer lead his fighter group. His future will be decided at a later date.

"You may stand at ease, Haeberlen," said Peltz. I remained standing to attention and replied that the Reichsmarschall had in front of the parade in Vels called me a "Cowardly Pig," and I intended to apply for an officer's honor process against cowardice in the face of the enemy. A change was noticeable in the attitude of the two officers. "If you do that it can cost you your neck." My short answer was,

"Gentlemen, has my officer's honor been defamated or not?" Annoyed, von Brauchitsch said "We will see what can be done in this matter. Please wait here until we return. You will be served a midday meal, and in the meanwhile we will return to Obersalzberg."

I was given an excellent meal, together with a bottle of French wine. Was this my "Gallows last meal?" I asked myself. I could not really believe that. How could a front line commander be penalized for saying what he thinks when it is based on fact, apart from a transfer to another unit? I had just finished the last bite of my meal and emptied the bottle of wine when the two officers returned. I again stood to attention and waited to hear the latest move. "An officer's process against Major Haeberlen will not take place. The remarks of the Reich-Marshall were made in heat, and will be seen as if they had not been spoken. The removal of your command remains. Your group is on parade in Hoerrsching. Colonel Peltz will fly with you there and make known the reason why you are departing." It seemed that the two were now concerned about me, sine they said that they would find a suitable position for me with regard to my flying ability and experience. Peltz, who had flown from Ainring in his Ju 88, now flew me to Hoerrsching. On the approach I could see the group on parade. Captain Unrau, the oldest captain, reported to Colonel Peltz that the 1. K.G. 51 were on parade. Peltz took me by the arm, pulled me to him, and said "On the order of the Reich Marshall, I must tell you that your commander is ill and can no longer remain in his post. Major Haeberlen has the thanks of his superior officers for his work by the K.G. 51, and will now leave you."

There stood all my comrades, some looking bewildered, others grinning in Peltz's face. I took a pace forward and said "Comrades, I thank you for your efforts and wish you all the best for the future.

I turned so no one could see how near to tears I was, and Haupt drove me for the last time to the dispersal, where Papenfuss waited in the He 111 with the engines running. With a quick handshake I said goodbye to my crew, the officers, and Peltz. I could not imagine that this was the end of my flying days—I could not and would not believe it. "Let's go" I said to Papenfuss, and he flew me to Schleissheim, where I rang Col. von Buelow in the control tower and told him how the proceedings had progressed. "Such is fate" he said, and added that I should go on leave to my family until a new post was available. I drove to Liesel and Dagmar and explained what had transpired during the day. The following weeks we remained in Munich. My brother, Walter, was now a sergeant and stationed at the air academy at Fuerstenfeldbruck. He had completed pilot training and achieved the B 2 license. He visited us almost every weekend. In the meantime, I renewed the acquaintance of the cantine chief at the Memmingen airfield in order to boost our food supplies, which were in short supply. In this way my brother Wagge, who was so called by the family, was given properly balanced meals. He thought a lot of Liesel, and once over a bottle of wine said that should anything happen to me, "we can get married. I will be the first to reach the rank of general, anyway."

The weeks passed, but a new post for me seemed to be a long way off. Somewhat nervous, I phoned the air force personnel office in Berlin from the air force authority in Munich. The chief of the department turned out to be a prior squadron leader of one of my squadrons, now Lieutenant Colonel Poetter. "Piete, haven't you any use for me?" I asked. Surprised, he said "Are you still in Munich? You will hear from me very soon. I'll send a teletext to Munich as soon as I've found something suitable." Christmas drew nearer, and my brother came to us. I had organized a fat duck from Memmingen, which Liesel cooked as with magic. It was a pleasant meal. On 30 December there came a teletext, brought by a courier, from the air force authority in Munich. It said "Major Haeberlen is to immediately report to the air force field command XXVIII in Treviso in Italy, as the 1a." This, of course, did not please Liesel, but I followed the order without delay. The next morning I caught the military train to Italy. I was curious as to what awaited me there.

21

FROM FRONT COMMANDER
TO BASE "OFFICE BOY"

It was the first time that I had traveled over the Brenner Pass. From Munich via Innsbruck, the train traveled down through the Etsch valley to the next station, Verona, where I had to change trains. I had been in France, Poland, the middle of southern Russia, Rumania, and Hungary during the course of the war. Now I was in Italy. From Verona, the train traveled to Treviso. I had forgotten that it was New Year, which made me wonder when the duty guard said that for the night I would be accommodated in a guest room in the camp. My normal room would be in the ready by 08:00 hrs the next day in the staff building, which lay outside the camp. The guard showed me to the mess and then disappeared. As it was almost 19:00 hrs, I entered the mess expecting to see other officers who would be celebrating New Years. Much to my surprise, I appeared to be the only officer there. A steward came and asked if I had any requests. I asked him when the party would take place, to which he replied that the officers celebrated in their rooms. This was my first meeting with the differences between the front line and units far behind the front. I then requested something to eat and a bottle of Chianti. This was the only Italian wine I knew of, apart from the Suedtiroler, which I had come to know when on walking tours with my father. While I waited for the meal to be served, there arrived a doctor who ordered something to take away. He saw me sitting there and said that I was not expected so soon, since it was assumed that I would celebrate New Years at home. "We front soldiers seem to have a different understanding of duty compared to that here." I answered. He asked if he could invite me to celebrate in his room, otherwise, I would be sitting here all alone. "You can also eat with us." I accepted and went with the doctor to his room. Again, I was surprised to see such a colorful assembly. It consisted of the doctor, two officials, and four ladies who were probably secretaries or nurses, all in civilian clothes. I must have shown my surprise, as the doctor said " Now you can see what it is like for us." Those present were not amused when I said "If you are interested in my opinion, I am disappointed in that the comrades are not celebrating together as we did in the front line." There was plenty to eat and drink, which loosened the atmosphere. After a while, an attractive blond came and sat on my lap. I pushed her gently to one side, stood up, and thanked my hosts for the party and said "The way things are here is not 'my thing' in wartime. My comrades who died in action would turn in their graves if they could see how things were here." With a "Good night" I left them and went to my room. I had given the steward orders that I was to be awakened at 07:00 hrs and shown to my permanent room in the staff building.

I entered the building punctually at 08:00 hrs on New Years morning, and an orderly showed me to my room. The general lived, together with his staff, in a small old castle with a large garden outside the camp. It lay away from the traffic, with a view of the old church, which was not too far from Treviso. Treviso was a middle ages town with a population of about 20,000 residents. Venice was also not too far away, and could be reached by car in half an hour. I had barely had time to look around my room, which had a view of the garden and contained a camp bed, a small table with chairs, a cupboard, and a large writing desk, when there was a knock on the door. In answer to my "Come in" a thin private appeared and said "Major, I am responsible for your well being, what can I bring you for breakfast? Chicken, scrambled eggs, and bacon, or..." At this point I interrupted him and said "Come here." I stood up and shook hands with him. The private, Richard Ambach, had such a strong handclasp that I found myself sitting in my chair again. I told him to sit down, as well. He looked surprised, which seemed to be prominent here. I learned that he was the manager of the general's mess. In civil life he was the owner of a well known wine tavern in Düsseldorf with the name "Ambachs Wein Tavern." I said "thank you for the generous breakfast offer, but I only want coffee, rolls, butter, a slice of sausage meat, and fruit. When you have something special, let me know." I also added that an honest soldier was more acceptable than one who concentrated on smartness and order. A few minutes later he brought my breakfast, and I asked him if he had a few minutes to spare, as I wanted to know more about the staff officers here. He answered all my questions, and in this manner I was prepared for the forthcoming meetings.

Ambach said that everyone was curious about the "Knights Cross" holder, since I was the only one there who had seen active service. He had described the staff officers, especially General Mahnke, the commander, very well, as I was to find out. Although it was New Years, I reported to the general at 11:00 hrs after his adjutant, Lieutenant-Colonel Mueller-Klemm, had explained the routine to me, which as 1a I needed to know. He was, incidentally, the publisher of the "Essener-National-Newspaper," a respected paper in Germany. It can be compared with the present newspaper, the FAZ. General Mahnke was a tall Prussian type officer. He received me in a friendly manner. He seemed to be pleased that he had a front-line air force pilot on his staff. He hoped that we would work harmoniously together, and that I should go with him to lunch in the mess, so that he could introduce me to the other officers.

The dining room was on the ground floor of the building and could seat 20 officers. The staff officers were assembled in the anteroom. He introduced them in rank order. Colonel Gottschling, Lieutenant-Colonel Bierfelder, the 1b (supply), the legal advisor Schwehling, Major Maier the 1c (security), Major Freund (intelligence), Staff director Huber, and Lieutenant Kurt von Tannstein the ordnance officer.

Private Ambach was standing behind the general and gave a sign to two Italians in white coats, who proceeded to serve the meal. The wine was served by Ambach personally. Mineral water was on the table for those who did not want wine with their meal. The food came from the staff kitchen, and was prepared in the mess kitchen by a cook, then supervised, and improved, by Ambach. Ambach's mother was born in Italy, the daughter of an Italian general. She came to Düsseldorf when she was 18 years old, where she met Ambach's father. Ambach could speak faultless Italian, which helped him to buy Italian food. He then combined Italian foods with the food from Germany, and so produced excellent meals. The wines were also excellent, due to his knowledge when buying.

My immediate superior was Colonel i.G. Gottschling, a typical staff person. He came from the Austrian army and was taken over by the air force during the occupation. He had no experience of air fighting and was a mere desk tactician. We never developed a feeling of comradeship between us. The field air force staff unit controlled all the air force airfields in Italy and supplied them with everything that was needed to function efficiently. These airfields operated from northern Italy against the English and American Mediterranean fleets.

On a visit to one of these airfields I met up with Gerd Helbig. We were students together in Lechfeld. He was now a squadron commander and wore the "Knights Cross with Oak Leaves" medal, and he later earned the "Sword" which went with it. Our quiet East-Prussian had gone further than a lot of other students. After the war he became the director of the "Berlin-Kindl-Brewery," a well known brewery. Also controlled by us were the units in the Dolomite mountains, who combated the partisans who were active in the region. They were led by English officers who were dropped at night by parachute. Weapons also arrived in the same manner. Counter intelligence was also controlled through our unit by Sergeant Rausch, who was a highly intelligent man and was a professor at Bonn University. He was often together with me, Major Maier von Tannstein, and Ambach during the evenings, in a room where we swapped stories over a glass of wine. One story told by Rausch was quite interesting. He had cracked the English secret communications code for submarines. With false orders he caused an English submarine to go on land in Venice, whereby agents were caught. He warned me about Gottschling, whom he trusted only as far as he could throw him. Now and again we invited Lieutenant-Colonel Mueller-Klemm to join us, but his manner was a bit too reserved and he did not really fit in with us.

In addition to my normal duties, I was given the pleasant task of accompanying General Mahnke during his visits to the outlying units and to conferences in a Do 217. I was very pleased, even though I recognized that with my "Knights Cross" the general was showing off a bit with me as "Chauffeur." Sergeant Vogt had, until now, flown the general. In this way I came to know all the airfields, such as Villafranca, Ghedi, Airasca, Lignano, Vicenza, Galarate, and Bologna. Whenever possible, I drove a Ferrari sportscar from the motor pool, to which I as 1a was entitled. It was the first sportscar which could reach more than 160 mls per hour. On some roads I really opened up, until on a hump backed bridge, just before Piacenca, I almost rammed a farmer who pulled out on the other side of the bridge in front of me on a tractor with a mowing machine. I learned from this, and from thereon reduced my driving speed. Sergeant Rausch sat next to me. He approved of my quick reaction, but requested that I drive less aggressively and slower.

One day, the 1a was requested on the phone. I answered, and to my surprise, on the other end was Lieutenant Colonel Dierich. He had been given command of the counter-intelligence unit operating against the resistance groups. He rang from his operations room and requested two or three anti-aircraft guns as support for his group. This I refused, and detailed my 1c, corporal Rausch, to explain on the phone how resistance groups were to be combated. As fate would have it, his unit came under our control, so I was now his superior, so to speak. I was in a position to give him orders, but I resisted the temptation. Major Mayer told the story during the evening meal, which brought a laugh. As our unit would soon be closed down, I had no opportunity to find out how long and with what success Dierich carried out his command.

There are three incidents that occurred in Italy. One was that the problem of supplies became more difficult due to the actions of the American air force, in that there were no longer usable bridges over the river Po. One would have to assess the situation on the spot to see what could be done to ensure the continuation of supply routes. To this end I was ordered to take a driver and a sergeant from the quartermaster's unit and find out exactly how and how long it would take to repair a bridge which could take rail and road traffic. As we came to the main bridge, we found that both rail and road had been badly hit and were not usable. I had to find a way to get my car over the river. Then I saw several fishing boats tied up to a small pier. Next to them sat the owners. As I requested them to ferry me and my car over the river, they demanded payment. I offered them about 500 Marks if they would tie two boats together, with planks laid on the boats, and take me over. They agreed, and within a short time we were on the other side of the river. I then promised to pay the same sum if they would wait for my return, in about six hours. Again, they agreed. We drove to a pioneer regiment and discussed the repair of a bridge for rail and road transport. Equipment that they did not have I would have to obtain in Treviso. We returned to the fishing boats. The fishermen lay relaxed in the shadow of the boats. As it was becoming dark and we were in the middle of the river, an American Lightning aircraft appeared over the horizon. These were very fast fighters, but luckily the pilot did not see us. We landed on the river bank, and I paid the required sum. I asked the men what they intended doing with so much money. The oldest fisherman said that he would not have to work for a week, and he then invited us to a Trattoria in the village, where we celebrated with chicken and rice and, of course, much red wine. We were not allowed to pay, as we had been invited. On the return journey I thought over what a German would have done in the same situation as the fishermen. He would have probably put up a sign on the road saying "Car ferry over the river Po" and made a lot of money. The people who lived here were happy with their simple lives.

I flew with Tannstein in a "Fieseler Storch" aircraft to a conference at the air force staff headquarters. This aircraft could land and take off on a football field, and I often flew trips in it. At the beginning of summer I had obtained an "Africa corps Uniform," with short trousers, short-sleeved shirt, black tie, and a white cap. This became my standard uniform. As Tannstein, dressed in the same manner as myself, reported to the 1a—a colonel i.G.—for the conference, it was obvious he did not approve of our dress and eyed us disapprovingly, but said nothing. After the conference, we were invited to the mess for a meal, but before hand we had to "borrow" the correct uniform from comrades there. This was long blue trousers, since our shirts were apparently OK. The commander was von Richthofen, whom I had "cut up" on landing in Soporoshje. In the meantime he had been promoted to Field-Marshal. Tannstein and I sat opposite him at the table, together with other high ranking officers. The marshal looked at me and said "Haven't we met somewhere?" I explained where and how we had met. He laughed and said "Gentlemen, listen to this," and proceeded to relate the story of our encounter. The meal was excellent, and as Richthofen finished his meal, the steward asked if he wanted more. He said "No thank you." All his staff followed his example and refused more. The steward was about to leave when I said that I would like a further portion, and my comrade, as well. Von Richthofen remarked to his staff "here sit two sincere men, for due to my stomach problem, I cannot eat a lot. As I refused more, you also refused more, although I know that you would like to continue eating." He could assess men very well. Smoking was now allowed, and everyone lit up except Tannstein and myself. "Don't you smoke?" asked von Richthofen. "Yes," we answered, "But the 'National' Italian cigarettes that we receive are not of the best." Richthofen asked to be shown one. He lit it and spat it straight away out. "That is dried horse dung. Don't you get anything better?" he asked. We answered in the negative. He then ordered his general manager to make sure that we were given good cigarettes. We thanked him, and with a few thousand cigarettes of a top brand, we flew back. Richthofen's death was sad; he died from a brain tumor before the end of the war.

On 20 July 1944, all officers were assembled in the mess anteroom. We waited for the appearance of Mahnke and Mueller-Klemm, scheduled for 12:30 hrs, and they were usually punctual. Ambach came and said that they would arrive shortly. There had been a serious occurrence. Eventually, over an hour late, they appeared with a serious expression on their faces. They said that there had been an assassination attempt on Hitler's life, which he had survived, uninjured. "Three cheers for the Führer," everyone cheered. We then sat down to our meal. The general asked me what I thought about it. He specifically asked me while I wore the "Golden Hitler-Youth Badge" on my uniform. I asked who was responsible for the attempt on Hitler's life, and was given the answer "a certain Major, Count von Stauffenberg and Major General Beck are the leaders in this affair." I replied that I knew von Stauffenberg, he was a friend of my cousin, Colonel iG Schmidt, who, as a divisional commander, was killed in action a short while ago in Russia. I would really like to know what these gentlemen had in mind, with this action. There was an icy coolness at the table after my comments, and the meal was eaten in silence. Tannstein, who sat next to me, said that I had stirred up a hornet's nest. Only the quartermaster and the 1c, Major Maier, attempted to revive the conversation. The army justice advisor looked at me with cynical amusement. A few days before, after an evening in the mess where I had drunk a few glasses of wine, he had asked me why I always addressed him by name, although we were both majors and he was senior. I then asked him what rank he had held during training. He said sergeant, whereupon I said that in the future I would only address him with his surname and leave out the "Mr." He never forgave me for not regarding him as a "full" officer. I had not been long at my desk after the midday meal when the phone rang. A voice at the other end said that I had to report, as the accused, to the Court-Marshal for trial at 14:30 hrs. I believed that the justice advisor thought he could revenge himself on me in this way. I called Tannstein to me, and we discussed how the situation could best be handled. I appeared promptly at the trial in the correct uniform. In front of me sat Schwehling, and at the sides sat two military legal men and two clerks. Schwehling asked me to explain to the court my remarks at dinner, in the presence of the general and other officers, regarding the cowardly assassination attack and the meaning behind them. As Tannstein and I had agreed, I gave the following in answer. I explained to the court that in my view, high ranking officers should think further before asking such questions. I was not the one who said what the others were really thinking. I had stated my opinion only. Somewhat angrily, the judge said "Case Dismissed," and I was a free man again. I was greeted by Tannstein, the 1c Maier, Rausch, and of course, Ambach. They were all pleased with the outcome. We celebrated in Major Maier's room that the legal advisor had shot in the dark and missed.

Von Tannstein and myself became quite close friends. He had been a diplomat in civil life and was now a reserve officer. His last position as diplomat was as Legation Secretary to the Vatican, in Rome. Previously, he had held a similar position with the ambassador, von Hassel, in Rome. Shortly after 20 July, Von Hassel was arrested in connection with the attempted assassination plot and hung. Tannstein was quite open with me and said he was against Hitler's politics and the party. I could not understand, however, how as a Protestant he let his two daughters be christened in the Catholic faith. His explanation only became clear to me at a much later date. He was of the opinion that on the collapse of all civilizations, the catholic church with the Pope would be the only institution to survive. The opportunities for Catholics in this world were better than for members of other religions. Time seems to have proven him right.

At the end of August, our unit was closed down due to the advancing enemy. All our commitments were taken over by the unit in Munich. It happened so quickly that there was hardly time for a farewell celebration. Only with close friends was there a celebration. In my room were: General Mahnke; Lieutenant Colonel Mueller-Klemm, who offered me a job on his newspaper "The Essen National" as a foreign correspondent after the war; Major Meyer, who invited me to buy early potatoes with him in Italy; Lieutenant von Tannstein; Corporal Rausch; and our now promoted Ambach. After a rather sad evening, we departed to other units. General

Mahnke parted with the words that I should retain my open-mindedness, but I should not get myself into unnecessary danger. "There are people who don't forget, so be a little restrained with them, and say nothing." Weeks later I visited my old Squadron Commander Poetter at the personnel department of the ministry, and I was able to see the last sentence of my assessment made by Mahnke. It said that I was an individualist and an able subordinate officer. Tannstein and I had to report to the "Front Pilots Collection Point" at Quedlinburg. Together in an air force truck, we went as far as Bozen, and from there we traveled with the Brenner mountain railway as far as Innsbruck. Nearby was Igles, where Tannstein's house was. On the way from the station to his house, he took me by the arm and said that he had something to tell me. "Mr Haeberlen, what I tell you now is impossible for you to tell to anyone else. Now that you are coming to my family, and home, I can tell you that for years we have hidden a Jewish friend. During the evenings, she comes from her cellar room to us upstairs. I know that we can trust you." The family had a large house, with a wonderful view of the mountains all around and a pretty garden. The guest appeared for the evening meal. She was a highly intelligent woman, and we discussed many topics, which lasted well into the night. I was very thoughtful as I went to my room, and I could not sleep for a long time. Why shouldn't normal officers who were fighting this war not know the things that I now knew? My experiences since the beginning of the war were leading me to re-assess my position with regard to the regime. The Jewish lady and Tannstein warned me to be very careful and not to put myself in any danger, as it was often better to remain silent. At the breakfast table, I asked Tannstein what he would apply for when he was in Quedlinburg. To my surprise, he said that he would ask for command of his old fighter squadron. He would be able to fly again. I then asked him how he could, as a fighter pilot, fight when he was against Hitler and the regime. "I will not fight for Hitler, but for my country," he said. There spoke the descendant of an old Bavarian officer's family. I had further reason to think deeply. Tannstein was later an Ambassador to Mexico, where he was active during the Olympic Games which were held there. I did not go to Quedlinburg, but to Geislingen, where Liesel and Dagmar now lived with my parents after our marriage on 12 April 1944.

My parents finally accepted that my marriage to Kaethe was a mistake. My mother visited Liesel in Munich, where they soon became good friends. My father arranged the divorce from Kaethe. He came to an agreement with her lawyer, so that there was no enmity in court.

There was a lot of paperwork associated with marriage. The family book, for instance, where ancestors were recorded in the minutest detail. There could have been a "Non-Aryan" included, which was against the Party rules. I laid all the necessary paperwork before Gottschling, who muttered under his breath. I explained my attitude towards titles and position in society.

Two days later I flew to Munich to get married. Sergeant Vogt piloted the Do 217, and we landed at Munich-Riem. After we left the registry office after the ceremony, we wanted to travel on the tram to my sister's home to collect our baggage. Liesel's mother had gone to Geislingen with Dagmar the day before. Suddenly, the air raid sirens sounded. I stopped the first air force truck that was leaving the city. I put Liesel in the driver's cabin and stood on the running board and held on tightly during the journey out of the city. I ordered the driver to drive through Bogenhausen, where we left the truck. The all clear sounded, and I phoned the air force unit and requested a car to bring us to the railway station. From there we went to Geislingen, which was for Liesel an unknown area.

After a relaxed celebration where, apart from my parents, only my brother Wagge was present, my father said "I'm afraid that we won't be able to celebrate in this manner for much longer." How right he was. Liesel was accepted by the family. She had a particular understanding with my father. The next morning, I reported by phone to Quedlinburg that I would contact the air force ministry personnel department under Colonel i.G. Poetter, who would give me a transfer.

A few days later the order came that I was to proceed to Rangsdorf, near Berlin, where I would report to the office of the "General of the Bomber Pilots" Lieutenant Colonel Marienfeld, who was stationed there, as he had requested me as his adjutant. This I saw as a sign of his trust in me.

22

FROM STAFF TO STAFF UNTIL THE END OF THE WAR

One day after I was given the order to join Marienfeld as his adjutant at the "General of the Bomber Pilots" unit in Berlin, I took the night train there and then the underground to Rangsdorf. The air raid alarm had sounded in Berlin, so there was no traffic movement. I made my way to Liesel's sister's home on foot. Both Friedel and her husband, Bruno, were surprised to see me, especially as during an alarm they and their neighbors went to the air raid shelter. They did not believe me when I said they could leave the shelter. I had heard the detonations in the north of Berlin and knew that the B-17's targets were there and not south of Berlin. I also heard the heavy flack explosions in the north, too. I stayed with them until the all clear was sounded and then made my way, via the underground rail, to Rangsdorf. As soon as I arrived, I reported to Marienfeld. Our meeting was very cordial after a long period of separation. After I had viewed my room, I collected Marienfeld and we went to the mess, where I was introduced to the other members of his staff. The 1a was Colonel Major von Beust. Marienfeld and I had a lot to talk over. He spoke of his time as commander, and I told of my "meeting" with the "fat one" and the results thereof. As he had to fly early next morning to Giebelstadt, we turned in rather early. On the first day, I was busy with my new job and responsibilities. The position of adjutant had been vacant for two weeks, so there was a lot to do to catch up to the present. I was about to leave the office and go to the mess at 20:00 hrs when the phone rang. I received the tragic news that Marienfeld, at a demonstration of a new aircraft machine-gun, had been fatally hit by a bullet and died immediately. A technical failure was the cause; a stay had broken, which caused the gun to swerve and Marienfeld was shot. During the course of the war, he had survived uncountable operations against France, England, Yugoslavia, and Russia, and now this. Horrified, the comrades heard my news in the mess. Everyone was saddened by this occurrence. An abyss opened up in front of me. Only the previous evening we had made plans, and now it was all pointless. But duty is duty, and I had to prepare myself for a new chief.

For the time being, Colonel von Beust took over Marienfeld's duties. We had a good understanding, and I found him to be a well balanced person. He had fought in Spain as a squadron leader in the "Legion Condor." Unfortunately, he was only temporarily attached to us, so he would soon be transferred to another unit. The next candidate was Major Storp, a successful commander and wearer of the "Knights Cross with Oak leaves," which he earned with the sinking of an English warship. He was an enthusiastic person who was simply full of ideas on how to run the war. We laughed at his "brain storms," so it was not surprising that we did not see eye to eye, so I had to forfeit my post. Our unit was ordered by the air force staff to move to a fighter pilot's school in Ansbach. Storp asked me to organize the move and come with him.

In the days following Christmas 1944, I had the opportunity to help my brother, who had phoned me in the middle of the night. After completion of training at the Air Force Academy, he was transferred to a fighter squadron in Jueterbog, where operations were carried out in an area east of Frankfurt on the Oder. On one such operation he was to attack Russian tanks, and unfortunately he was hit and had to make a belly landing. He hid in a concrete waste pipe on a bridge, with the intention that when it was dark he would find his way to the German lines. Suddenly, he heard voices and thought that Russian soldiers were in the near. Then he heard an unmistakably annoyed expression that could only come from Schwaebische soldiers. He looked out of the pipe, and made himself known to a patrol from the Schwaebische Regiment. They took him to their headquarters, and from there to Frankfurt, where he took a train to the Potsdam station, in Berlin, from where he phoned me. After some discussion, I arranged to meet him in Rangsdorf. He was not a pleasant sight to behold. He was very dirty, and his clothing was torn. The first thing he needed was a bath and fresh clothing, including flying boots and overalls. When that was completed, we went to the mess, where he was given a meal and a drink. He reported to his unit in Jueterbog by phone and explained the situation. I requested from his squadron leader that he spend a couple of days with me to recover from his experiences. On the evening before his return, he played cards with our master players, both meteorologists, who played skat. After the first game they suggested a high stake. Wagge then won most of the games and collected quite a sum of money. I was reminded of my mother's advice when I joined the army, not to play any card game for money. As a young girl she had seen a young officer in the family fall deeply in debt due to playing cards. He was persuaded to go to America to avoid the consequences. He was only to return when he could stand on his own feet. In those times things were very strict. The next morning I arranged for Wagge to be taken to Jueterbog, where he flew more operations and succeded in shooting down two B-17s.

The Formation Leader School was also transferred from Tours to the Ansbach airfield. The commandant was my old friend Teddy Schwegler, who was with me when I was with the K.G. 51. In the meantime he had been promoted to major. Our meeting was very amiable after so long. The reasons for the meeting, however, were not so pleasant, as we realized that the war was lost. Although I loved flying, the air force, and my officer's career, I was bitterly disappointed at the way in which the German people were told to hold on, and at the same time saw their cities devastated and the advancing Russians who murdered, raped, and plundered in East and West Preussen, Pommern, Schlesien, and Mecklenburg. The reports which landed on my office desk were shattering, to say the least.

With all this in mind, during our move to Ansbach, which was via Jueterbog, I found Wagge's fighter group. I wanted to discuss with him the way the war was going. In a room of the airfield commander's, I waited for Wagge to appear. As soon as we were alone, I came straight to the point. "As your elder brother and in my position in the G.d.K., where I have access to secret information over the front-line activities, I must tell you that it seems pointless to fight further, as the war is lost. Now, as a sensible person you should avoid risks and seek to protect your family as well as possible. Your commander has told me that you will soon be transferred to an airfield in the south, near Bayreuth. There, you will be relieved of the task of holding up the Russian advance, to allow the refugees to make their way westwards. The Americans have crossed the river Main and are advancing on the Main valley. In a few weeks the war will be ended. Through criminal direction from the 'top' only disaster is programmed for our people. Believe me, it is not worth giving your life to support these bandits."

Even today, I can't get over his reaction to my little speech. His only words were "Up to now I did not realize that my brother was a traitor." He turned and left the room. I often attempted to phone him, but he never answered. On 20 April, as he was on a landing approach at an airfield in Oberfraenken, his aircraft was shot down from above by an American Thunderbolt. He is buried in the war cemetery near Vilshofen above the river Donau. He was a young man blinded by the party propaganda, brave and willing to fight for his country. He was never a "War Criminal," which now stamps his generation.

Deeply hurt, I went back to Ansbach. The newly found acquaintance with Teddy was not to be of long duration, because an order for my transfer as Officer z.b.V. to the air command V 11 in Munich lay on my desk. This commando had its operations room in the Scheyern monastery near Pfaffenhofen, on the river Ilm. There I met only "behind the lines" officers and was again practically the only officer who had front-line experience. The commander was General Vohrwald, an affable person, although our first meeting was not so affable. It so happened that I had just arrived at the unit and was on my way to the mess. I had to pass by his accommodations, when, at that moment, a truck unloaded a refrigerator and several boxes of wine, which were taken into his room. He came out of his room and I reported to him. I gave my rank and name, and said that I was transferred to his command. I then asked him if he thought that in the present war position, it was a good idea to refurnish his quarters, especially in view of all his subordinates who were quartered in nearby barracks. He seemed rather taken aback, and he looked at me, but said nothing. When I arrived at the mess a further surprise awaited me. I asked a steward to bring me a drink. "What would you like," he asked, "beer, mineral water, or a glass of wine." I looked at him in surprise and asked if they had all this here. He answered that such drinks were only for the officers and the civil servants. I ordered a glass of red wine and asked him to point out the mess manager, if he was present. He indicated the gentleman concerned, and I made my way to him. Having made myself known, I said that it appeared that a discrimination existed between the officers and the men in the supply chain. "I am going to ask General Vohrwald to change this at once. Do you believe that by the front-line fighters, to whom I recently belonged, in their difficult operations, often with heavy losses, there is a difference in the supply between officers and men? The situation here is scandalous, to say the least." The mess manager was flabbergasted at my onslaught. To say that I was the most loved member of the mess was overdoing it a bit. But as a "Front Liner," I just had to explode.

I had hardly had time to accustom myself to the new situation when orders came that the complete unit was to move to Holzkirchen, south of Munich. The American troops were advancing swiftly. With every day they came nearer. During the transfer, I had a duty car, driven by gas. I made a few trips to Geiselingen, where I left most of my baggage, including my flight book and action reports. I asked Liesel to hide the documents in a safe place so that the advancing Americans would not find them. She chose to hide them under the mattress on Dagmar's bed, thinking that the G.I.s would not search there. During the journey over the Schwaebisch Alb to Ulm, the driver and I were often attacked by aircraft, and had to seek shelter by hiding under trees or elsewhere out of sight. We were not detected, and arrived at our unit in Holzkirchen. It was not long before the G.I.s occupied Ulm. I suggested to the general that, if it was possible, we discharge the men who lived nearby from the army, so that they would not become prisoners of war. The discharge dates could be back-dated. The general said that this was something he could not decide, and I should seek permission from the air force control south. I phoned them, and spoke to the general commanding. I made my suggestion and received as answer, "Major, do you want to betray, in the last days and hours, your loyalty to our Führer and commander in chief, Adolf Hitler?" I could not understand his position, and said to the effect that I was loyal, but if the possibility existed to save men from prisoner of war camps, I would undertake this on my own responsibility. End of conversation. I lied to General Vohrwald, saying that the air force control south had given us a free hand. I was also able to persuade the headquarters chief of staff that concern for our men was more important than stupid "hang on" sayings, in view of the overall position in which we found ourselves. In four or five days the G.I.s would overrun our position, and it was time to think what one was to do to avoid capture. It did not take long for them to make up their minds, and so far as was possible, the necessary papers which showed that they were discharged were given to the soldiers who could make it home. It still is not clear to me to this day why so many high ranking officers did not see the reality of the situation, or would not accept the fact that we would be completely defeated. A few days before, my driver drove me to relatives who had a farm near Rosenheim. My uncle was a professor of agriculture, and experimented with ways to improve yields. He was the inventor of the green feed silos which are to be found anywhere where dairy farming is carried out. He also worked with the "Gervais Trust" to establish what methods were needed to achieve the highest fat yield in milk. The farmhouse had a large attic, and there I hid sausages, fat, and conserve tins. Under the floor, I hid 12 bottles of Henessy cognac. My intention was to hide here as long as it was necessary. The dispersal of our unit proceeded quickly, and with the remaining officers I shared what remained in the "war fund" cash box. During the night I took a BMW motorbike and packed my rucksack full with my escape goods and civilian clothing, and drove to Bad Toelz, where a rest home for fighter pilots was. There I met a few old acquaintances, comrades who were relaxing from their operations against the enemy. One such was Major Peltz, and another was my previous squadron commander in K.G. 51, now a commander of a torpedo group. We were all of one mind, that it was time to organize a safe hiding place in order to avoid capture. The manager of the home gave me a "Robot." This was a camera, with which we took photos of our missions with the Ju 88. At that time, it was an expensive camera. I then drove to the Bad-Aibling airfield and gave the airfield commander instructions to make available the quarters of the single officers, which were all empty, to the local people before the Americans came. I was continually amazed by the way some officers wore blinders, in that they could not accept that Hitler, who had brought the army and the people much worry, would not end the war.

In Rosenheim I ordered the air force supply depot to be opened for the people. There was some protesting from the guards, which I settled by drawing my pistol. I was almost a victim of this "Hold On" fiasco. Shortly after leaving Rosenheim, I came to a control point manned by S.S. men. Of course I had the necessary movement order, which said that I had to deliver an important message to a unit in Wasserburg. My "Ritter Cross" was visible on my chest, but my rank badges I had removed before going to my uncle's farm, so that I would not be recognized as an officer by the workers there. I was allowed to drive further without any problem. Anyone who experienced those times will realize what a close shave that was, especially as in my rucksack there were empty army pay books, several different army passes, and duty ink stamps. I was prepared for eventualities. One never knew when they would be needed. At the entrance road to the farm—Haiming, it was called—I left the main road and drove through a wood that was a few hundred yards from the farmhouse. I stopped in the wood and hid the motorbike in the bushes where it could not be seen from the road. I then removed the number plates, stowed them in my rucksack, and walked the rest of the way on foot. I knocked on the door, which was opened by my uncle's manager. He recognized me and let me into the house. He advised me to change into civilian clothes as soon as possible. There were two workers on the farm, both prisoners of war; one was a Pole, the other an American. At breakfast it would be explained to them that during the night a bombed out engineer, who was related to my uncle, had come from Munich. My aunt Marthe and my uncle Karl had expected my arrival. I settled myself in the attic, which was only entered by climbing a steep ladder. I had just gotten into bed when the manager came to me. He suggested that in the morning I dress in the worker's clothes which he had brought me, and come to him so that he could give me a job to do which would allay any suspicions the two prisoners of war might have. I then explained to him where the motorbike was hidden in the wood and asked him if he would hide it in the barn under straw, from where at a later date I would collect it when the turmoil of the occupation was over. This he promised to do, and to keep his mouth shut. I gave him a substantial amount of the money I had with me, which would help him to sustain his family after the occupation.

At 6:30 hrs the next morning I went to the manager's house, where I breakfasted with his family and the two P.O.Ws. As he was responsible for feeding the complete farm personnel, he had decided to slaughter a pig and a calf. The meat would then, eventually, be stored in tins. The Polish P.O.W. was also a farmer, and the manager gave him the job of slaughtering the animals. The other P.O.W. and myself were to help him. He, his wife, and the maid would also help. As the slit the calf's throat with a large knife, the thought went through my head, what would he do if he knew that I was a German officer. My throat, as well? Luckily, the two looked at me as a normal worker. As the days went by I took my cue from the manager. I heard on the "Enemy Radio" that the Americans had captured Munich and were advancing along the Munich/Rosenheim highway. That we would soon be in the net was obvious. I did not think there was any danger to the farm's occupants from the two P.O.W.s. I thought that they would say that they had been well treated. But suddenly the situation changed completely. As soon as firing was heard in the distance, the two P.O.W.s left the farm. We parted amicably, but they wanted to be free and went to meet the advancing troops. Dusk was falling when two German army vehicles, a car and a truck, appeared at the farm. I went straight away into the house, and my uncle opened the door. He was told that they had become separated from the rest of the troop, and would like to spend the night in the barn. The group consisted of a captain, a 2nd lieutenant, a staff sergeant, two sergeants, and three soldiers. In the farmhouse on the ground floor was a large dining room with a built on bay which led into the garden. In the hall were doors to the kitchen, work room, and to my uncle's and aunt's bedroom, with a bathroom. A permanent resident was their daughter, Brigitte, who was half paralyzed from polio contracted in her childhood. As guests at the farm were my sister, Hanna, with her two children, Mulle and Peter, and my brother in law, Kurt Ziegler. He was also an old comrade from the time in Memmingen. Unfortunately, he had injured his leg in a crash with a W 34 (an air force training aircraft) so badly that it had to be amputated. He was wearing civilian clothes, but no other evidence to show that he was an invalid and not a soldier. My uncle had invited the officers to dine with us, which they accepted. They sat on either side of my uncle, while I sat at the opposite end of the table in my working clothes. During the meal I said nothing. I was introduced to the officers as a nephew who had been bombed out in Munich and now worked for him. Now that the two P.O.Ws had left, my uncle's manager was glad to have help with the farm work.

I made a mistake after the meal was ended, in that I smoked one cigarette after another. This was unusual, as cigarettes were practically unobtainable at that time. I was on the way to the toilet when I heard steps behind me, and a voice said "so, you are a deserter." As I turned, the captain stood there with a drawn pistol pointed at me. I said "how do you know that, captain?" My right hand was in my trouser's pocket, and with my left I knocked his pistol out of his hand and drew my "Walther

PPK," which I had by me ever since I worked at the farm in civilian clothes. "Captain," I said, "you have made a mistake. I am Major Haeberlen, group commander of a bomber group. You, and your men, will leave this farm in the morning." I then showed him my army pay book that I had with me. I then sat at the table again. I followed the conversation between my uncle and the officers. The captain was in civilian life a high school director in north Germany, and during the war was with a unit that was now retreating, which meant that they were thinking of deserting. My uncle left the table, and the officers joined their men in the barn. The men had been given a meal in the kitchen. I explained the situation to my uncle, who said he would be glad to see the last of the visitors. If G.I.s showed up at the farm it was better if they did not find any army personnel there.

The captain and his men left early in the morning, as agreed. Some five hours after they had left, we heard heavy machine-gun fire. I ran to the door and saw a fanned out formation of American armored cars advancing over the fields. They were firing in the air, as a warning. I gave instructions that we should hang white bedsheets out of the windows. I then ran to the attic and changed into my uniform, with the "Knights Cross" visible. I asked Kurt to change, as well. As the Americans approached the farm, we all stood by the door. They belonged to a Texas tank division. With my hands in the air, one hand holding my pistol by the barrel, I stepped forward and said "Please, here is your new prisoner." They checked that both Kurt and I had no concealed weapons on us, and they also checked the contents of my rucksack, but did not take anything. We were taken to a truck, and Kurt had to be carried, as he was not wearing his prosthetic. My sister, aunt, uncle, and cousin had tears in their eyes as we were driven away. The G.I.s took my "Knights Cross" away and fired my pistol a few times in the air. They seemed pleased with such a capture. We were on our way to prison, which I had wanted to avoid. The G.I.s paused in a wood. A captain came to me and said that they had captured a German captain who had told them that a high ranking officer was to be found at the farm in Haiming. He had even showed them on a map where the farm was. Kurt and I looked at each other aghast. So much for "Comrades." This captain had betrayed us, and I did not even know his name. We now knew what to expect in the future, and as P.O.Ws. above all we must exercise caution. The Americans drove further, but it was not long before they made another pause and started to celebrate with whisky. My "Knights Cross" went from hand to hand. It did not take long before they were all in a drunken sleep. I asked Kurt how far he could go on crutches, if we ran away. He said that if we did run away, they would soon catch us, as we could not travel very far. So we waited until they recovered, and we drove further.

23

PRISONER OF WAR AND RETURN HOME

We were brought to a barn next to a sports arena in a village. This was to be our temporary prison. In the barn were various ranks and units of the army. I asked some of them to make room for the disabled Kurt, only to be given the answer that for them the war was over and I had no authority over them. A couple of sergeants stood up and dealt a few telling blows to the miscreants, and they then made room for us by them in such a manner that during the night we would not be disturbed. The next morning we had to parade outside the barn. Amongst the prisoners were two young Waffen SS men. They were taken into a wood behind the barn by two guards. We heard two shots, and the two guards returned alone. It appeared that not only the army had committed atrocities. The two young men were murdered without a fair trial.

An American sergeant, who spoke almost accent free German, told us that we must walk 20 miles to a prison camp at the Aibling airfield. The sick and wounded would be transported in a truck, and should step forward. The sergeant went along the lines to check that no one was trying to sneak a ride instead of walking. As he stood in front of Kurt, who supported himself on my shoulder, he asked me what reason I had not to march. I explained that I must stay with my brother in law to help him. He then said that they would look after him. I then said "Sergeant, I have been ten years in the air force as pilot and probably never walked more then two miles, so must I, at the end of my military career, walk so far?" He said OK, I could travel in the truck. Again, I had proved that it was best to be quite open when dealing with G.I.s. After a short journey we arrived at the Bad-Aibling airfield and were taken to a hangar where several hundred officers were accommodated. We were given a bed with only planks as a mattress, on which three people had to sleep by the "Senior Officer" who was a lieutenant-colonel. In the hangar the officers were divided into groups of 100 to 200. My brother in law Kurt had wisely left his prosthetic at home. After two days he was allowed to go home. We were rationed to one slice of bread and a small tin of meat or fish per day. Hardly enough to keep flesh and bone together. The G.I.s received much more. Several young officers made the mistake of consuming their whole ration in one go, and then had to wait 24 hrs for the next ration. Quite a few collapsed due to hunger. I had the daily task of reporting the number of men in my group who would receive rations. I had upped the number by sixteen so that we were given a bit more. I had ordered that young officers up to the age of 21 receive more to eat. One officer, a 2nd lieutenant, had reached his 22nd birthday. I told him that he would no longer be given extra food. The next morning I was dozing on my plank bed when two armed G.I.s appeared and took me to their officer, Major Rollin. He sat in his office with his feet on the desk and said "I have received a report that you, Major, have made false reports regarding the number of rations required for your men." I asked how he knew this, and he mentioned the name of the 2nd lieutenant who had reached his 22 birthday and would now only receive the normal food ration. "Major Rollin, if the situation was reversed, wouldn't you do the same for your hungry men?" "That's right, major," he said. He then changed the subject, and explained that there were some 60,000 landsmen on the airfield. The prisoners were divided into 15 groups. For the group number 14 he was looking for a group commander, and he asked me to undertake the position and establish order in the group for the benefit of the soldiers. As I was hardly in a position to refuse, I accepted the post. "You will continue to live in the officer's hangar. Your duties will commence early in the morning and last until the evening. A captain will explain your duties to you."

In one way, I was pleased to have responsibility again, instead of wandering aimlessly about in the hangar. I began immediately with the organization of the group. First of all, I ordered some 20 staff-sergeants and sergeants to divide the soldiers into sub-groups of 200 men. In my group were some 4,000 men, all mixed.

After my "Knights Cross" was taken from me, I had the E.K.11 order, which hung on a short chain, converted into a "Knights Cross" with the help of comrades, complete with half a hanging chain that another comrade who also possessed the "Knights Cross" had sacrificed. I could now wear it every day.

Within a few days I had group 14 organized. Soldiers built showers with water pipes that we obtained from Major Rollin. All the tents were lined up in rows. Between the tents were gangways, and through the middle of the rows of tents was a group road. For the rubbish, holes were dug in the ground. The captain who had explained my duties was satisfied with my efforts. One day we were paid a visit from General Patton, who was the successful tank commander of the U.S. forces in Europe. A couple of sergeants had selected a very thin man and laid him on a wooden plank, with the intention of showing the general the results of the meager rations we received. The general actually did visit my group, and saw the prisoner and the rations. He was indignant, and as the man responsible for the rations was in his entourage, he told him what he thought. The man could only stammer "yes sir, yes sir." The next day all prisoners received a greater amount of food.

The next morning I went along the group road accompanied by a sergeant and saw three soldiers lying in the sun. Next to them lay paper, empty tins, and other rubbish. I said "Comrades, you know that rubbish should be put into the holes specially dug for this reason." "The time for braided officers is over," they said, and made no effort to carry out my instruction. The sergeant blew his whistle three times, and there appeared our group's police. Discipline must be enforced with so many men. The three were taken away. Our group court consisted of a staff-sergeant, a sergeant, a corporal, and two privates. They sentenced the three to three days on half rations for refusing to carry out an order.

One evening, as I sat on my plank bed, there came two G.I.s who brought me to Major Rollin. "Major, are you a Nazi officer?" he asked me, and continued by saying that a member of my group 14 had complained about me in that I did not treat the soldiers correctly. A door opened, and one of the privates, whom I had ordered to pick up the rubbish, appeared. Before I could say a word, he produced from his pocket a book which showed that he was a member of the communist party, Germany, and had been for many years. "Major Haeberlen, you can go," said the major, surprisingly. Before I left I requested that I be relieved of the post of group commander. I had done my best for the soldiers, and if that was the thanks for my efforts to establish order, I saw no reason to continue. Rollin agreed, and then asked if a good cook was to be found in group 14. "When you have found one, then I will find a successor for you."

I asked around in the group for a cook, and an elderly sergeant reported to me. He came from Riedlingen, on the river Donau, and told me that at home he had a butcher's shop with a guest house. Then he divulged to me that his wife and five children waited for him to return. He had been a member of the "Waffen SS," which no one in the camp knew, and had the number of his blood group tattooed on his upper arm. This was common practice with the "Waffen SS." Now the contents of my rucksack came into question. I produced an army pay book complete with the appropriate stamps. I advised him to work in the American officer's mess, as cook, because there he was less likely to be checked.

I gave the sergeant cook's name to Major Rollin as suitable for the job in their mess. Before he reported, however, I took him to one side. I took him in the officer's hangar, and I told him that a doctor there would be able to help him get rid of the tattoo. The doctor made two incisions in the shoulder and cut the tattoo out. In an army pay book that we made to look older, he noted a wound on the shoulder caused by a bullet. A few days later Major Rollin came to me and thanked me for finding such a good cook for his mess. He then added that the German communist who had reported me was put on a train to join freed Russian workers in a camp. There was only one thought in my mind, what would happen if he ever returned and sought me out. I thought, however, that he and the other workers would be put behind barbed wire for brain washing. I heard from the cook that he survived the war without any problems. He thanked us that we had helped him, and had pushed food under the fence for us. I now began to collect the food necessary for my escape.

Six weeks went by, and we heard that our release was near. The camp's American officers had been relieved, and a new group took over. Instead of a front line tank officer as commandant, a Colonel Rothschild now occupied this post. His staff were, without exception, all German Jewish, and they spoke perfect German. One morning, all officers had to parade in front of the hangar. A Lieutenant Rosenfeld then said that all officers who had occupied control positions should step forward. I made the mistake of stepping forward, and was taken into a special tent, which was rather high. Around the tent was high barbed wire. There were three-tier beds, wooden, of course. I was directed by the oldest officer, a Major i.G Mueseler, to a bed on the top tier. The bed was next to the tent wall. Next to me was a lieutenant from Tuebingen, who confided that he was with a propaganda unit, and therefore especially in this tent. Altogether there were about 80 officers, mostly staff, propaganda, and intelligence men.

After the first night, it was clear to me that I had to get out of there as soon as possible. We were guarded by colored G.I.s, and one afternoon I spoke to one of them. I showed him my aircrew watch, which I had kept hidden in my jacket, and said that if he let me crawl under the fence I would give him the watch. He examined the watch and said "O.K., you second class person, I also second class person. Tonight at 3 o'clock, be here." That the lieutenant would also accompany me, I did not mention. As a well disciplined soldier, I reported to Major Mueseler that two officers would be missing from the morning parade. "But major," he said, "You can't do that, it will cause difficulties." I then asked him if he was going to betray his comrades. He did not answer. The lieutenant and I waited for the appropriate time and, undetected by the other comrades, we left the tent. The 2nd class comrade had kept his word. He was given the watch, and we crawled under the fence and mixed with the prisoners who were to be released the next day.

Very early the next morning, the release procedure began. In the hangar where we were previously, six tables stood in a line, and at each one was an American officer. I was wearing my "Knights Cross" and my rank badges, together with other decorations, on my uniform. As I came to the table, I laid my pay-book down with a picture of Liesel with Dagmar sitting on her lap uppermost. "That's a pretty blond girl," said the officer. "That is my wife and daughter," I said. He looked up at me and asked "Nazi?," to which I replied "Yes." He shouted over the other tables "Boy, here is the first Nazi." He took a thick book which contained the names of wanted Nazis from the party, special units, SS, and SD. Of course, he did not find my name amongst them, since I was never a party member. My activities as a bomber-wing commander did not interest him. "How come you are the only Nazi" he asked me. "Lieutenant," I said, "I swore an oath to serve Adolf Hitler, which as a soldier I could not break without being liquidated." "Well, that's OK," he said, and stamped and signed my release papers. Further evidence that one should be open when dealing with G.I.s.

With the long awaited release papers in my hand, we were taken to a place where the transport vehicles were assembled. All ex-prisoners were squeezed like sardines into the trucks and driven to the zones now occupied by the Allied forces. Comrades from the Russian occupied areas could also join their relatives in the west. We spent another night in the open and, naturally, it drizzled. We sat close together for a bit of warmth, as it was a cold night. Before we were allocated to a truck, a Sergeant Moser told us to remove all rank badges and throw them in a heep on the ground. As this was completed, he said we should do the same with our medals and orders. A stillness came over the assembled men. I took my "Knights Cross" from around my neck and threw it at the sergeant's feet. "Don't do that," said the comrades, but I said, turning to the sergeant, "There, now you have the orders." He said that I could keep my order, but I said I would not bend down to pick up rubbish. The rest of the men now threw all badges and orders to him, so that he stood knee deep in them. Many thought that the sergeant would be angry, but he ignored it all and produced a list which detailed which truck was destined for which town. As he said "Truck to Goeppingen" I said "that's for me," and climbed aboard. Shortly thereafter, again like sardines in a tin, we drove off. The driver was a colored corporal who drove very fast through Augsburg to the exit in Dornstadt near Ulm, which meant that he made good time on the journey. There was very little civilian traffic on the motorway, but considerable military traffic. Over the Schwaebische Alb our driver did not let up, and we continued to make good time.

We drove through Geislingen, but I did not see anyone I knew who could have informed my family. In the center of Goeppingen we stopped, and the corporal said we should alight. I attempted to ask him if he would drive me as far as Geislingen, as it was on his way to the motorway. I got no further than "Please corporal" when he interrupted me and said that I should speak German. "In America I am studying Germanistic," he said. I said that my father would have a bottle of Cognac or Schnaps for him if he drove me there. With an OK and a laugh, it was settled. I sat next to him in the driver's cabin, and he actually drove me to my parent's doorstep. Liesel lived there with Dagmar and her mother. I was glad that I had been able to get my mother-in-law out of Berlin in time. Incidentally, my corporal had a book by Hoelderlin under his seat in the truck. He held Dagmar in his arms, said "Hello" to the family, and received his bottle of Cognac. He then drove off into the darkness.

It was a stormy reunion with the whole family. They were all happy that I was back home at last, and with valid release papers. Now nothing more can happen, I thought, the war is behind me. This, of course, was tempting fate, as I was soon to find out. My mother came to me in a nervous state and with a serious expression on her face. She said that the communists were in control in the town hall, and when it became known that I was there, I would be arrested. "You must disappear from here and live low." I was disappointed, to say the least, and I certainly did not want to be a prisoner again. We discussed where Liesel and I could go. I had decided that we would not be separated anymore. In the weeks as a prisoner, I had imagined everything to be quite different, but the danger was too great. After a while, we decided that in the morning we would flee over the hills behind us.

24

ESCAPE TO HAIMING AND RETURN TO CIVILIAN LIFE

I told my family of my experiences since I was last at home late into the night. A few days before, a squadron comrade who was passing through Geislingen on his way from POW camp to home threw out a message from the transport, which was given to Liesel. She knew from this that I was alive. We decided that it would be best if we went quickly to Haiming, where there would be room for us at my uncle's farm until the situation had cleared.

At 4 o'clock in the morning, while it was still dark, I crept out of the house and made my way to a high lying plateau in the Alb. I had a well packed rucksack with me, and I waited there for Liesel, who had to de-register and collect her ration card for the next period. I would never have dreamed that I would have to leave my home in the middle of the night, like a thief. In the POW camp I had to suffer a few setbacks, as well as the denounciation. We had also seen how our comrades from Austria suddenly separated from us and hoisted their flag. Only a short time ago we flew as comrades together against the common enemy. I had much to learn about people and their reactions. A great disappointment came over me as I sat in the early morning on a rock and looked down on my home in the valley. Was this the thanks for all the fallen comrades? There had been no news from my brother Wagge since April. I slowly came to learn that many people lied about the past. Everyone was against Hitler. It was not just the hunger behind barbed wire that made denounciation and opportunism prevalent. Hours later Liesel arrived, together with my mother. A quickly built wagon to carry our baggage did not last long on the stoney ground. They had to shoulder the packs when it collapsed. We must both carry our baggage now. It was another parting from my mother who, with tears in her eyes, watched us disappear over the brow of the hill in the direction of Ulm. My mother was a very helpful and socially oriented person. During the war she had helped where she could. In the winter of 1941 she had collected warm clothing for the east front. At the railway station she had provided food and drinks for the soldiers and refugees the entire night. Needy families were also given food and drink. All this caused my father to complain that he was neglected, but she was in her element. She was extremely disappointed by the outcome of the war and the defeat of Germany, because she had believed it was a good cause. Just a few days after we had left, my mother was arrested because she was a member of the NS-women's association, which helped anyone in need. She was at that time 56 years of age, and was taken, together with high ranking officers and generals, to a tented camp. She sought out an American captain who seemed to be in charge, and in English explained her position, and asked him if he thought it was fair to punish people who had only helped others. Within a few hours, she was on her way home.

Via side roads we reached the village of Lonsee, where we spent the night at a farm, the owner of which was a friend of the family. The next morning saw us on a milk float, which took us to the motorway Stuttgart/Munich lead-on at Dornstadt. Liesel played the "Blondy Girl" to hitch a lift on the motorway to Munich. It was not long before an American truck stopped, and after examining my release papers, we were allowed to climb on it. Without further stops we reached Munich, where we again stayed with friends. At about 5 o'clock the next morning we set off for Rosenheim. Again, a milk-float took us through Rosenheim. We continued our journey on foot through fields and wooded footpaths. After some two hours we reached Haimimg, where a moving reunion took place. In the meantime, other members of the family had also arrived at the farm, seeking security. These included my sister Hanna and her husband, Kurt. From my aunt's family, her daughter-in-law, Ursel, whose husband, Major i.G. Juergen, was killed in action. On the way she had met a Willi Arent, and together they battled their way to her in-laws. Willi Arent was known as "Lotter Willi," and was before, and during, the war a salesman for the firm of Henkel, which produced a washing powder known as Persil. In Berlin he lived well. We soon discovered that he was a smart businessman. He was given his nickname from the fact that, as he could not have a room in the farmhouse, he had partitioned off a portion of the upstairs hallway as his room. Behind the partition there was a continual rise of cigarette smoke. He got up in the mornings when the others were busy at work. He never helped at all. He did nothing, but always had cigarettes and alcohol. Where he obtained it all was for us a mystery. He often rode on a bicycle through the nearby villages. We liked the way he got on with people in a very uncomplicated way, especially with my aunt and uncle. He was always polite, but distant. From the north came, unexpectedly, my aunt's niece, Suse Knauer, along with her two daughters. In addition, there lived with us a Mr. and Mrs. Rothenbuecher, whose home had been destroyed by bombs and had evacuated to the farm. For us, only the flour storeroom was available. We had only one desire, and that was that we would never be separated again.

So that we would not be a drain on my uncle and aunt, we decided that we would distribute the housework. The harvest had been gathered in, and we began to glean the fallen corn. By sunrise we started, and continued until 11 o'clock in the evening. We had stiff fingers because the temperature was not very high. Later, with stiff backs, we returned with our sacks of corn. Then, all we could do was flop out on the mattress, since we had no bed, and sleep. One day Liesel sprang up and said that Dagmar had arrived. Through the window we could see Lene, Liesel's sister, with Dagmar in her arm. The end of the war had found Lene as a telephone operator in Czechoslovakia, from where she traveled—partly on foot and partly by hitch-hiking a lift whenever possible—to Geislingen, where she could live at my parent's house. She knew that her mother was living there, It had only taken her, and Dagmar, two days to travel to us. We were again a complete family. Lene went back to live at my parent's home shortly after. Liesel and I imitated the squirrels, in that we collected pine cones in the forest, since it would soon be winter. For this reason we could not live much longer in the attic, as there was no heat up there. We moved into a large room in which Hanna and Kurt had lived with their children. They had gone back to Munich to live in their home again. Kurt had been given, due to his injury, a student's place at the technical university. Now my hidden bottles of Cognac came to light. I swapped two bottles for a good tiled oven, with which we kept our room lovely and warm. We burned the pine cones we had collected, and they gave out a good heat. I was given a ration-card after I obtained a job with a building firm in Rosenheim. I worked on the renewal of the drainage pipes. My hands after two weeks were so blistered that I got an abscess on them, which meant that I could not work anymore with a pick and shovel. In the meantime, the foreman learned that I could carry out writing and other work. From then on I controlled the movements of the various building machines, and also the road traffic with a red and a white flag. I ordered the necessary material, and was a Jack of all trades. After six weeks my abscess was worse, and it had to be cut out. This meant that my job as a builder's laborer came to an end.

Lotter Willi had left the farm and gone to Stuttgart a while ago. He let me know that he could use me in his newly established firm, and to this end I should contact him. Liesel hitched a lift in a jeep as the first step on her way to Stuttgart. I watched her leave with some trepidation, as I stood with Dagmar in my arms on the main road. After five anxiety filled days, she returned with a work contract for me as a commercial businessman in the firm of "Wiro GmbH," which was the name of Arent's firm. Liesel had also looked for a flat in Geislingen, and told me the glad news that we could return there.

The move to Geislingen had to be organized. The corn that we had collected we took to a mill, where it was ground, and we ended up with a hundredweight of flour. This also had to be packed, together with things which we had collected in the time we spent at Haiming.

Everything that one needed to exist was achieved illegally, since the Reichmark was worthless. Cigarettes were the "money" in those days, and everything had a set value in "Chesterfields" or "Camel" cigarettes. For instance, a packet of American cigarettes could be exchanged for a half pound of butter, then one pound of butter for a bottle of Schnaps. This situation continued until the new money was available in 1948. Thereafter it was possible to buy goods in the shops, although some things, such as butter and milk products, were in short supply until 1950.

The move was completed without a hitch. We brought everything with us to my hometown. Two American officers had their quarters in my parent's house for a while. As soon as the room became vacant my parents moved into it. Most of the valuable furniture had been removed to the hotel Sonne, which housed the American officer's club.

Then the house was confiscated, and filled with displaced persons from Estonia who had fled from the Russians and were waiting for their acceptance either in the United States, Canada, or Australia. My parents had to live in father's office. Grandmother Prill and Lene were given accommodations by neighbors. Liesel and I arrived in Geislingen and had nowhere to live. I went to the housing authority office in the town-hall, where I was given another surprise. As a result of the influx of German refugees from east and west Preussen, Pommern, Schlesien, and the Sudatenland, as well as the confiscated houses by the Americans, the housing authority now controlled the rest of the available homes. As I asked if there was anything available for my wife and daughter and myself, I was refused with the explanation that I no longer had the right to live in Geislingen anymore. I then asked why, and was told by a young office boy, with a communist badge of the communist party (KPD) on his jacket, that war criminals were not welcome in the town. Then came the helping hand of fate. My father had, during the war, successfully defended the man in charge of the housing in a court case. He was now in a position to help my father, which he did, and we were given attic rooms with a family of our age. One day before Christmas our second daughter was born. We decided on the name Suse for her. Our attic flat was not only too small, but during the severe winter Liesel's bed, which was against an outer wall, was frozen. When the warmer weather came, the plaster on the wall broke off. We then moved to rooms in a house belonging to an elderly woman who was not well disposed towards us, especially Liesel. We had to share the kitchen with her, which was a source of trouble. In other ways, as well, she made life hell for Liesel. In the end Liesel's mother came and stayed with us. She had to sleep on the settee, but made sure that the landlady did not go too far with her complaining. Then she turned her attention to me and spread the rumor that I dealt on the black market, and often brought things home in the middle of the night. I spoke to her on this point and said that if she did not stop making these false accusations, she would find herself in court to face a slander action. She then screamed at the top of her voice, so everyone could hear, that I came good out with lawyers, from whom I had learned my deviousness.

My father issued a complaint against insult at the court. She did not attend the hearing, but even so, had to pay the court costs and my father's fee, as well as a sum of character damage to me. We found another flat, again in the attic, and the removal expenses were paid from the character damage money I had received. This flat was very large, but without a bath. During the cold weather it was difficult to keep warm, so most of our time was spent in the kitchen.

At this time the "de-Nazifying" procedure was taking place, and although I was never in the Nazi party, I was accused of being a Nazi, since I had, during 1933 and 1934, organized the German Youth in the town between 8 and 14 years of age, and had received the "Gold Hitler Youth" emblem for my early membership. This had nothing to do with politics, except that the kids were true to Hitler. It was purely a youth organization. Most Germans favored Hitler at that time, which is shown in the results of the elections in 1934. This election was the last in the "Third Reich," and 45% of the electorate voted for Hitler. The question is "why?" The late history professor Hellmut Diwald writes in his book "History of the Germans" on page 185f a plausible answer. The most serious question in Germany at the end of the 20s was not which government succeeded the previous one, but was the new government capable of solving Germany's fate and furthering the power of Nationalism, or not.

There is no doubt that not one of the republican or democratic parties in the Weimar period made the effort. They were blinded by the national dissatisfaction under which millions of Germans had suffered since 1918.

The government takeover by Hitler in 1933 was in accordance with the constitution. It showed the will of the voters, and it was more democratic than any government since Bruening. 52% of the voters stood behind the government.

As I was well known in my home town of Geislingen, the courtroom in which my process was to be held was full. I sat alone at the defendant's table. My lawyer had passed his final school exams three years before me, and then studied law. Because of his poor health he had not been accepted by the military.

As the so called judges panel entered the courtroom, everyone, except me, stood up. I remained sitting. The panel consisted of members of the KPD, SPD, FDP, and CDU. The chairman, who was previously a military judge, asked if the accused was present. I said "Here," but remained sitting. He then asked me why I did not stand up when the judges panel entered the courtroom. "You are a panel set up by the Allies. For me your decision in this case is not valid." Then I stood up. The questions they asked me were laughable. Then they asked me if, as a pilot, I had ever bombed civilian areas. I answered with a question, "Had you gentlemen not seen Ulm or Stuttgart near at hand, the centers of which were totally destroyed by bombs?" As a defense witness came my old 1a, 2nd Lieutenant Fritsch, who was not affiliated to any political party, and was now a professor and director of a commercial school. In his evidence he said "Major Haeberlen was the only officer to order his subordinates to do that which he himself would do. He was the most liked commander that we had, and he was constantly concerned with our well-being." Then a letter from Kurt von Tannstein was read out, in which he said "Major Haeberlen was one of the officers who was often critical of Hitler's regime, so long as it did not endanger his life." In any case, I was fined 2,000 Reichmarks. As I left the courtroom, the communist from the panel asked me how I was going to pay the fine. I answered that I must sell a carton of American cigarettes. He looked a bit bewildered, and wished me luck. This gentleman moved to the Soviet Zone, where he was given the post of "Peoples Judge." He returned to the west before long, greatly disappointed with communism as practiced by the SED, and he approached my father for help. Two days later he was found poisoned in his room. In the police report was the remark "Murder by persons unknown," although anyone abreast with the political scene could sense that the hand of communist security was involved.

After my temporary job in Stuttgart, I joined a course to become a textile salesman in a large weaving firm. I reported to the job-agency and was asked my trade. I said "Major and Pilot," and was told that that was no longer a trade. I replied that he would be glad to earn as much as a pilot. Then he said we should not argue about it, he knew that I had passed my final school exams, which meant that I could count. Therefore, he would list me as salesman, which I later was. With my 30 years it was difficult to find a place as a student, because none of the cowardly citizens wanted to employ a previous youth-leader and pilot. The director of the south-German cotton industry in the nearby town of Kuchen knew our family well. My father had arranged that the Jewish director come onto the board of directors, together with the NSDAP representative who, of course, did not want to damage his position. In this way the Jewish family was secure for the entire Hitler period.

Now that I was ready to sign the agreement for the course, there came a political hurdle. I was automatically given the entrance forms for the trade union to sign. I refused to sign, and the secretary said in that case I could not start there. I asked to see the firm's union boss. He was an old school comrade of mine. He had returned from a Russian POW camp in good condition, since he had joined the National Committee for Free Germany, a Russian organization for socialist oriented Germans. "Is this your form of democracy, to persuade me to join the union when I do not wish to?" I asked him. His face turned a red color, and he approved the course without my joining the union. I had made a dent in the front of the union. When I left the firm eighteen months later, half of the workers were no longer in the union.

After learning spinning, weaving, color, and film printing, I moved to the sales department, where I commenced to study the bookkeeping system. While the others there helped me considerably, especially with difficult tasks, the senior bookkeeper was different. He made me understand that what he said I had to carry out without question. As I was given unimportant tasks to do, I spoke to him on this point. When I asked him if he had no desire to teach me anything, he said "what can one expect from someone who wears a 'Knights Cross.'" I grabbed him by the arms and took him to the window, which I opened and said "Take that back, or I will let you drop." He stammered an excuse, and from thereon he made sure that I learned. Apparently, my action had made the rounds, and I was treated with respect after the incident.

I also had to attend the technical school classes. The other students were 16 or 17 year old girls, which was the normal age for apprentices. I was elected the class prefect. By the class outing, I was allowed to smoke and drink a glass of wine. Learning the course material presented no problems. My course was shortened to eighteen months due to my age, after which I took, and passed, the exam set by the chamber of industry in Goeppingen. I was now a fully-fledged textile salesman.

I was in the sales department of the firm, and my sales area included Essen and Wuppertal. My wages were not high. In the beginning I received 129 D-Marks for the month. Thirty Marks a month went to rent. We, Liesel, Dagmar and Suse, had to exist on the rest. Needless to say, it was hardly enough to keep body and soul together. After six months I received an increase of 51 D-Marks. In the end my wage was 210 D-Marks. It became clear that I must do something to earn more money. I contacted a friend who had served as technical officer in my squadron in Stuttgart. He said he would help me to find a well-paying job. Then my situation in the factory changed.

One morning the oldest expert was called to the director. He soon returned, mumbling under his breath "What do they expect, in the direction." Shortly after the next was called, and so on, depending on the length of time one was in the firm, until, just before the midday break, I was due. The chairman, the sales director, and the firm's lawyer were present. "Mr. Haeberlen, you know that our representative in Wuppertal, Mr. Kretzmann, cannot carry on the business and has given it to his wife. This morning we received the news that she has been admitted to hospital. We would ask you if you are prepared to go to Wuppertal and present to the customers our new collection." Naturally, I was ready, and how! If the gentlemen thought it was necessary, I could travel on the evening train Munich/Dortmund, which left Geislingen at 20:30 hrs. "If you give me the collection, and time to pack, I can be on the way there." The director said that I would travel in two days time, but I should first explain everything to my wife. I said that she would be overjoyed when she heard the news.

Three days later I stood in front of the Wuppertal rail station. It, as well as the town, had been severely damaged by the bombing. Everywhere there were signs of recovery, and workers were busy erecting scaffolding and rebuilding damaged houses. I found a furnished room in a large house owned by a Jewish family. The man had a highly placed job with the town council. The next day I commenced with the display of my goods. With my display case and briefcase I was under way by tram and train, for weeks on end. I returned home just before Christmas, but kept my room in Wuppertal. The firm's management were very satisfied with my work, and asked me if I would take over, as a traveling salesman, the Wuppertal district. I asked for a contract to this effect, and after some discussion, it was agreed. My predecessor was unable to work, and his wife had recently died. I now looked for a house, as the job was permanent. The firm helped with a loan, which was necessary to buy a house. At Easter, the family moved into a house with four rooms in Wuppertal-Barmen. Liesel's mother came with us, as her house in Berlin no longer existed. She was a lusty person, and could look after the children, at times.

The firm had also provided me with a car, a DKW, which I needed to transport the ever larger collection. Four years later my father bought a house with a very large garden in Wuppertal-Kuellenhahn. It lay in the hills near a wood. For the purchase, he was given a building society loan. Over the years my sales area increased, due to the deaths of colleagues in Essen and Cologne. I earned good money and had a free hand, but a dream job it was not. The main thing was that I earned sufficient income for the family. In the Autumn of 1961, I commenced with the building of our holiday, and later retirement house, in Hagnau. It was to become our favorite holiday home.

I underwent an operation for a hernia in 1972, and thereafter I was forbidden by the doctors to lift anything heavy. As this did not pass with my work, I gave up my contracts, except for one in St. Gallen. I was given, thanks to a government law, a small pension, from which we could just about live. We decided to move into our house in Hagnau, on Lake Constance, or Bodensee as it is called by the locals. My mother had died at the age of 81, and Liesel had looked after my father until his death in 1982. The two had a good understanding. After a heart attack in 1989, we sold the house in Hagnau, and moved to a house in Friedrichshafen that we had bought.

Our life ran along normal lines ever since I had taken over the sales area in Wuppertal, so there is nothing more to write about.

My aim with this book was to show my life as a youth, during the war time, as POW, and life during the rebuilding of Germany, so that our children could form an impression of a life in these times. Long years with difficulties which, for the present generation, do not exist.

EPILOGUE

My story is not a documentary. The point that I have tried to bring out is to show the younger generation, who were born after the war, our life before Hitler, the war time, and the rebuilding period after the war. Maybe I have shed a different light on many aspects that are widely held.

Amazingly enough, no one was involved in, or part of, the Hitler period. The school teachers preached a history in which they did not believe, but it was so ordered from "Above." History was distorted to fit the times and aims of the Nazis.

We can see the same game in 1989 being played during the collapse of the DDR. The chief of the espionage department in the DDR, a criminal by the name of Markus Wolff, said that he was not guilty, and was strongly supported by the "Left" media.

Who can say that a difference exists between the Nazis of my generation and the communists of today, when the same crimes are carried out? Why do the media skillfully transmit programs dealing with the war in Serbia-Bosnia-Croatia and to help the raped women who are not allowed to return to their own countries? When was a voice with such intensity heard regarding the rape of German women by the Russians? Will the following generation have two standards, for friend and foe?

In the German parliament it was decided to rehabilitate all deserters, and a sum of money was determined for them. In the case of political or religious viewpoints one can possibly accept desertion. But to rehabilitate deserters who had left their comrades in the lurch should not be acceptable. It would not be acceptable in any UNO country. They should be looked upon as traitors.

By the swearing of the oath of allegiance by the young soldiers in Berlin, some 12,000 idiots shouted soldiers are murderers. These people were protected by the police. The soldiers must defend these idiots with their lives, when necessary.

My conviction is that one day the true historical facts will come to light. Why do the Germans listen to everything which condemns them?

After more than fifty years have gone by since the end of the war, I hope that my book presents a correct picture.

Anyone who has spent six years fighting on three fronts, has learned that in all systems and among all people, there are good and bad. The responsible people at the "Top" in any system, are never guilty of anything bad.

The author in traditional dress at the annual children's festival.

Left: The author, Klaus Haeberlen.

Below: The Haeberlen children, two sisters and two brothers. On the right, the author.

In the Austrian mountains, 1931.

As a youth leader.

1935. Cadet in the Third Prussian Transport unit.

1936. Drive from Berlin to Hannover in my uncle's American Auborne sports car.

The Do 23 two engined bomber in Lagerlechfeld.

1937. Start of pilot training in an He 72.

1938. A Do 17 flying over the Alps, on the occasion of the occupation of Austria.

1939. How I saw myself as a cadet at Werder.

1939. At the controls of a Ju 52 flying from Memmingen to the war college in Werder.

The new crew, 1941. From left to right: Observer Private Heinz Ernst; 2nd Lieutenant Haeberlen; Radio operator Corporal Bubi Boettcher; and gunner, corporal Michael Gallermann.

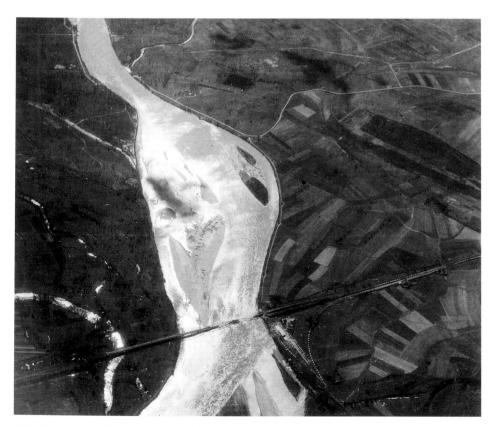

1941. Yugoslavia, the destruction of the Sawe bridge by the crew.

Dive-bomber Ju 88.

1941. A Ju 88 on the airfield at Lezany, Poland.

Ju 88s in a low level attack.

1941. Living in a tent on the airfield Vlodimierz.

Growing a beard.

1941. Balti-Ost. airfield. Exchanging poultry and biscuits for cigarettes and schnaps.

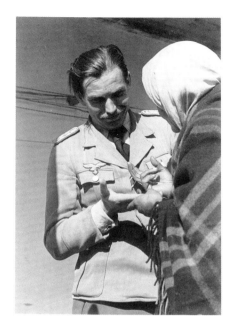 

1941.Balti-Ost. airfield, Gipsy dancing group visit. Dancing and horoscopes for bread and cigarettes.

1941. Ju 88 dropping bombs in horizontal flight.

24 September, 1941. Mass attack on the Russian headquarters in Perekop, Krim.

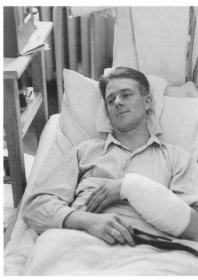

1941. Field hospital, Nikolayew.

March 1942. Captains Baumbach and Haeberlen.

1942. Attack on Black Sea docks in Tuapse.

Reconnaissance photo after an attack. Freighter and three submarines sunk.

June 1942. My 100th operational flight. Attack on the rail station at Kupyansk.

Congratulations after the 100th operational flight.

6 January 1943. Flack damage in wing of Ju 88 during attack on Semikarovskaja.

1943. In the severe winter, crew in fur clothing.

Inspection of a destroyed Russian tank.

17 April 1943. The 300th operational flight. Wearing a life jacket, required when flying over water.

Commander Major Kurt Egbert, talking to Captains Haeberlen (left) and Rath (right).

24 June 1943. At the controls of an He 111 during a flight from Bobruisk to Illesheim.

An Me 410 with rocket pods.

20 June 1943. Presentation of the "Knights Cross" by Squadron Commander Heise.

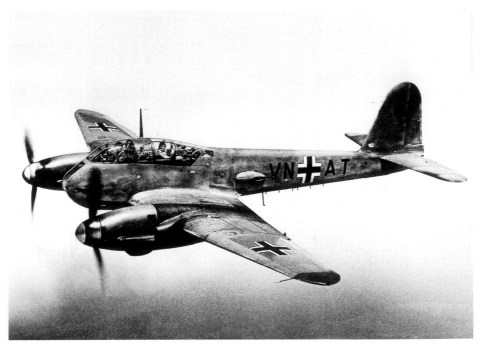

Messerschmitt 410 aircraft.

End of June 1943. Civil reception at Geislingen town hall for crew and technical maintenance man.

An Me 410 with technical maintenance man Corporal Seiderer.

11 October 1943. Reprimanded, and relieved of my command by Göring, also called "the fat one."

Springtime 1946. Thin from prison food, with Liesel and daughter Susanne.

2nd Lieutenant Haeberlen at the flying school in "Stieglitz."

Do 17 E in formation flight.

Lieutenant Haeberlen as Group Flying Instructor, in winter clothing.

The commander of the III./ K.G. 51,
Major Marienfeld.

Loading a 1,000 kg mine under the belly.

A Ju 88 A4 on the way to bomb England.

Officer's mess and accommodations in the Castle Écharcon.

Major Marienfeld by the Hunt.

Captain (Med) Dr. Ott and 2nd Lieutenant Capesius by the Hunt.

Group parade in Wiener-Neustadt on 20 April 1941, with Major Marienfeld and a rear view of Lieutenant Haeberlen.

The crashed aircraft of 2nd Lieutenant Maletz and crew after a low-flying accident during training in Hungary.

The funeral of Maletz and crew in Wiener-Neustadt.

Low-flying training over flat land in Hungary.

Air force chief Major General Loehr visits Lezany with Squadron Commander Lieutenant Colonel Schultz-Heyn and Major Marienfeld.

SD2 in low flying bombing attack.

Vlodimierz airfield.

Effectiveness of our SD2 low-flying attack on captured Russian airfield. Destroyed Ratas and a TB-3 bomber.

Group of gypsies on the airfield at Balti-East.

The 500th operation of the III./K.G. 51 with Lieutenant Haeberlen on the left.

A Ju 88 in formation flight.

Lieutenant Kielhorn's grave.

Lieutenants Baumbach and Fritsch, the group's 1a.

Left and Above, Opposite: View of docks and port of Nikolajev.

The freighter and passenger ship *Nikolai Ostrovsky* before the war.

The *Nikolai Ostrovsky* after the attack and being sunk by the author.

The rest-home accommodations for the III./K.G. 51, near Odessa.

Destroyed Russian tanks at Kupjansk.

Bombing hit on railway targets.

The 300th operational flight by Captain Haeberlen. On the aircraft's nose, the Memmingen town arms.

The 100th flight of Lieutenant Haeberlen against the enemy.

Cpt. Haeberlen and crew accompanied by the mayor, inspecting the lines of the youth organization.

Commander of the VIII./ flying corps, General Pflugpeil, in Charkov. On the right is Major von Bibra. On the left is Captain Haeberlen.